Seeing the Sun behind the Clouds

SEEING
the
SUN
behind the CLOUDS

A Weatherman's Faith
through the Storms of Life

Lacy Bernett Padgett
Betty Hendricks Padgett

TABLELAND PRESS LLC

Copyright © 2020, 2023 Lacy Bernett Padgett and Betty Hendricks Padgett

Seeing the Sun behind the Clouds: A Weatherman's Faith through the Storms of Life by Lacy Bernett Padgett and Betty Hendricks Padgett

All rights reserved. No portion of this book may be reproduced, stored in a retrieval system, or transmitted in any form or by any means, mechanical, electronic, photocopying, recording, or otherwise, without written permission from the publisher.

Published in the USA by

TABLELAND PRESS, LLC
www.tablelandpress.com
info@tablelandpress.com

ISBN 978-1-949323-08-5 (paperback)
ISBN 978-1-949323-09-2 (ebook)

Illustrated by Allison Chisum and Tiffany Gill.

Caricature drawings by Joe McKeever.

Photos or other assistance provided by Betty Padgett, Eileen Cooke, Margaret Sorensen, John Padgett, Rachel Harris, Allison Chisum, Stephanie Sorensen, Tiffany Gill, Marjorie Anne McGhee, and Mary Jean Padgett.

All scripture quotations are taken from the King James Version of the Holy Bible (KJV).

Printed in the United States of America.

*To my children, Eileen, Margaret, and John, with much love.
Without them, this book would not have existed.*

Contents

Foreword..ix
Preface...xi
Introduction: A Can-Do Attitude........................1

Part One
Bernett's Memoirs

1: Childhood Memories 5
2: Fun with My Cousins and Friends 11
3: At My Grandparents' House...................16
4: Easter Fun..................................21
5: Family Stories..............................25
6: Fishing....................................27
7: Animal Tales...............................30
8: Foxworth, Mississippi......................34
9: My Teen Years..............................38
10: College 44
11: Korea.....................................47
12: Ardmore...................................61
13: New Orleans...............................67
14: Huntsville................................72

15: Memphis. 76
16: Picayune 84

Part Two
Betty's Memories

17: Weatherman 93
18: His Faith 96
19: Mediterranean Trip 100
20: Just Routine 104
21: Life with Prosthetic Legs. 111
22: Alaskan Cruise. 118
23: Tippy 122
24: Going Home. 133

Epilogue. 139
Appendix A: "Sometimes God Calms the Storm" 141
Appendix B: "A Savior Came from Heaven" 143
Appendix C: "I'm Going Home" 145

Foreword

Bernett Padgett was a giant of a man spiritually—quiet and intelligent. He was a devoted husband and father who loved his God, family, and church. He also was very serious about his position as a weather forecaster. His interests included woodworking, gardening, and writing. Bernett loved planting trees around the yard and doing yard work. Even when he lost both his legs, he would get on his riding mower and mow the lawn. He wrote several songs, which his wife, Betty, set to music.

Though Bernett wasn't much of a talker, if you listened closely, he was very funny. One day I was eating lunch with Betty and Bernett at his favorite place—McDonald's. Betty and I were talking nonstop, and I asked Bernett what he thought about what we were discussing. He said, with his dry humor, "I never pay any attention to what you gals talk about."

Bernett never missed an opportunity to help others. Once (this was after Bernett had lost his legs), Betty loaned me a piece of furniture that needed some repair. Going to their house to pick it up, I discovered that Bernett had pulled it into the driveway and was sitting on the asphalt, doing his handiwork, making it like new. I was amazed that he never let anything stop him.

Before he passed away, he wrote many stories about his life. Betty and their daughter Margaret put Bernett's writings into a wonderful book. This is his story, and I know you will enjoy reading about his shenanigans.

—Frankie Willingham Wyatt
Author of *Now I Know His Name*
and *Preacher Willingham*

Preface

This tale began with my husband's childhood memories. As Bernett dictated, I sat at our computer and typed. He told about the mischief he had gotten into as a boy, his service in the Korean War, and the different places we lived while he worked as a meteorologist for the National Weather Service. When we finished, I sent a copy to each of our three children and Bernett's two sisters.

As a surprise to Bernett and me, our daughters, Eileen and Margaret, and son, John, along with granddaughters, Rachel, Allison, Stephanie, and Tiffany, collaborated to have the stories printed as a book. Margaret organized the paragraphs into chapters, edited them, and added photos and the illustrations drawn by two of our grandchildren. For Christmas 2014, they gave several copies to us.

After God took Bernett home, Margaret (who had started her own book publishing company) urged me to finish the story. I wrote several more chapters, which include not only Bernett's prolonged medical crisis, but also, with God's help, his determination to keep going in spite of having to use prosthetic legs. God was with us all the way through life's storms and helped us more fully understand the meaning of Psalm 46:10, "Be still, and know that I am God."

—Betty Hendricks Padgett

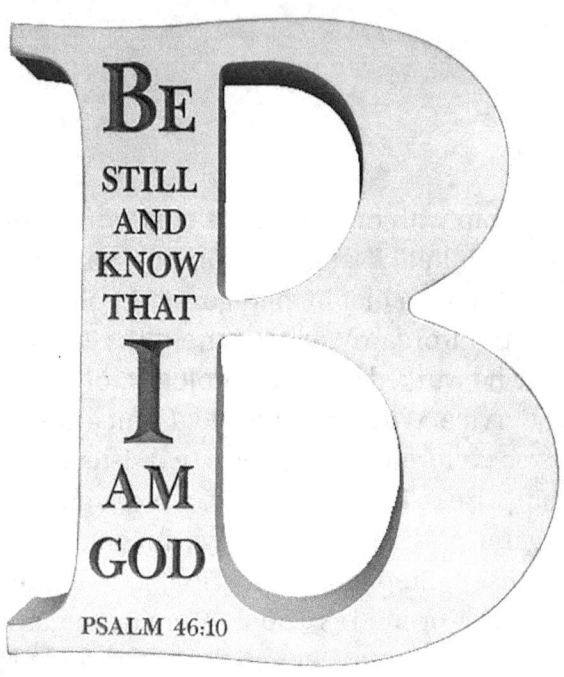

Introduction

A Can-Do Attitude

Bernett wondered why he was short of breath. It was January 2001, and the seventy-year-old man was used to being very active. Obviously, as he got older, he was slowing down some. But he had only been to get the mail! He and his wife, Betty, had recently returned from a trip to Oklahoma to visit her relatives, and Bernett had noticed that doing simple tasks now made him tired. For the past few days, after he had walked the short distance to get the mail or to take out the trash, his breathing had been quick and labored.

Bernett mentioned his concerns to Betty, and they scheduled an appointment with a cardiologist. After looking at the EKG, the doctor recommended an angiogram to see exactly what was going on.

On the day of the angiogram, Betty, their daughter, Margaret, and Bernett's two sisters, Marjorie Anne and Mary Jean, waited for the doctor's report. The doctor found five blockages in the arteries in Bernett's heart. Bypass surgery was scheduled for the next week.

Little did Bernett and his family know that this would be the beginning of a long ordeal that would end with both of his legs being amputated below the knees. God was going to test their faith.

Several years later, Bernett wrote his memoirs. He felt that he needed to share his experiences with his children and grandchildren. Surprisingly, or rather, not so surprisingly, he didn't mention his thoughts or feelings about having to walk with two prosthetics. He never really thought of himself as handicapped. He just took things in stride (pun intended).

After God called Bernett home, Betty decided that her husband's story should be shared with others. She added supplemental chapters to his memoirs to complete his narrative. In those chapters, she shared her thoughts and feelings about relying on God throughout her husband's medical crisis. She also described what it was like for him to live day by day using artificial legs.

As you read Bernett's memoirs and Betty's memories, may God bless and inspire you to never give up and to always concentrate on what you *can do*, rather than on what you *can't do*.

Part One

Bernett's Memoirs

Chapter 1

Childhood Memories

On a cold winter day (December 4, 1930), a son was born to Barney Evon Padgett and Mary Ludie Gill Padgett in a farmhouse outside of Magee, Mississippi. You did not go to a hospital to have your baby back then. You hooked up the horse and buggy, drove five miles to town, and looked up the doctor, who went back with you to your house to help with the delivery. Or you called on several of the ladies in the community who were experienced in helping with childbirth. I was given the name Lacy Bernett Padgett by my grandmother Nettie Aceneith Anderson Padgett. Lacy was her grandfather's surname. The name Lacy did not give me trouble up through high school but did cause me problems in college and the United States Air Force, where people are generally called by their first and last name. Even today, I receive mail addressed to Ms. Lacy Padgett.

My father was one of six children (three girls and three boys). Uncle Milton was the oldest, with Aunt Rosie and Aunt Rutha next. Then came Uncle Andrew (Skeet), my father Barney, and Aunt Oredus. It was nice to have everyone together at Thanksgiving or Christmas. Aunt Rosie's was the only family that did not own a car. She had all boys in her family—five of them. They lived around eight miles from Grandpa and traveled by wagon. They would start out early in the morning and arrive around ten or eleven o'clock; then after lunch, they would start home midafternoon. With the boys in her family and the boys in Uncle Milton's family, we had one big time playing.

My mother became pregnant again and had a baby boy. His name was Edgar Holcomb Padgett. He was born on September 29, 1933, and died on October 23, 1933.

When I was four years old, we lived in a house owned by Pa Turner. He lived just a short distance from us and had a small boy about the same age I was. One day I was taken to his house and told to stay there until they came for me. That afternoon when they came to get me, they said that I had a new sister. Her name was Marjorie Anne Padgett. She was born on July 23, 1935. Since I was four and a half years older, I was still boss. When she grew up, Marjorie Anne got her nursing degree in Mississippi and had a long career in nursing, first in New Orleans, and then in Magee, Mississippi.

I can remember when my father bought his first car. The price of cars then was $600 to $800. We did not have paved roads like we have now; there were only dirt roads with gravel on them. I remember that, several times, we slid into a ditch and had to get a mule to pull us out.

One time we were going to see Grandmother Hales (Grandfather Gill had died before my mother was born, and my grandmother had then married Pat Hales), and we had to go on a road that had deep ruts down the middle of it. Well, we got stuck and had to seek help to get out. We went back home another way to avoid the ruts. They have gradually paved most of the roads now, and travel is much easier.

We did not have electric lights, a refrigerator, a TV, or a telephone in my younger days. Grandpa Padgett finally got electric lights when I was around eight or nine years old. We had to use kerosene lamps for light, and we had an icebox in which a huge chunk of ice was put to keep things cold.

My younger years were generally normal. My father was a Baptist preacher, and in the early years, he preached at many different churches on a quarter- or half-time basis, before working up to full-time. During the week, he taught school; and during the summer vacation, he went to school to finish his college degree.

One of the first big things that happened in my young life took place while we were living in Hattiesburg, Mississippi. Dad was in college there, and we were living on the second floor of a building. I was riding my tricycle down the hall, when, somehow, my foot struck the floor, and I stuck a three-inch splinter into my foot. Boy, did that hurt! I had to be carried to the doctor who tried to remove the splinter but was only able to remove part of it. He said that, with time, the other part would work itself out. A week or so later, I was riding my tricycle, and I hurt my foot again. This time, the splinter came out, but it left a big scar.

I stayed with Grandmother and Grandpa Padgett many summers. During one of these summers, the next big thing occurred. Mother and Grandmother were peeling peaches on the kitchen porch. (The kitchen was separate from the house. There was a walkway between the house and kitchen. A porch, which was about four feet off the ground, ran along the entire width of the kitchen and eating area. Back then, houses were built this way to prevent the whole house from burning down if the kitchen caught fire.) They had a big tub of water that they washed the peaches in. When they were through with the water, they just dumped it over the edge of the porch. I was going to be a big boy and dump the water for them. The only problem was that, when I dumped the water, I went with it, fell in the yard, and hit a stob. I knocked a big gash on my head, so the old mule had to be hooked up to the wagon, and off to town we went to see the doctor.

My father was teaching school at Old Hickory (in Mississippi) when I became five years old. He thought that it would be a good idea for me to start school a year early. Although I would have to repeat first grade the following year, the learning I received this year would be a help to me. I started school, but going to class, I had other thoughts. I disappeared and could not be found. At noontime, the search began. I had found me a place of security. I was under the schoolhouse as far as I could get with my faithful dog by my side. They tried to get me to come out, with no success. Finally, they had to send one of the bigger boys to drag me out. This was my first day of school, which ended there. Another year passed before school started for me.

One day, before I learned to swim, they made a flotation device for me, and the entire crew went swimming in a pond near a house close to the church. The water was not clear but was okay for swimming. The device that they made for me consisted of a piece of cloth fastened between two empty syrup cans by their lids. Most everyone was in the water when one of the lids on a syrup can came loose, and down I went. One of my cousins, Doris (Uncle Milton's daughter), was next to me, and she pulled me out. My mother said that she was ready to go in after me. That wound up my swimming for the day.

We had a lot of fun after I learned to swim. About a half mile from Grandpa's house was a place they dug gravel from. While digging one day, they hit a spring of cold water, and the hole filled up with the coldest, clearest water that you could find. They put some trout in the water, which we could see swimming around. This is where we went swimming. You could not stay in the water very long because your fingers would shrivel up and your skin would turn blue. You had to finally give up and go home. But, oh, what fun we had in this swimming hole!

One day, we went to town and then started to go see Grandpa Padgett. It had been raining a great deal on the Okatoma Creek watershed, and when we got to this creek, the water was out over the road. A pickup truck had made it across just before we arrived. Well, Mother said, "Don't try it," but Daddy said he thought we could make it. Well, he drove off the bridge and into the water. It was deeper than he expected, and the car drowned out. Then began the job of getting us kids and Mother out of the car and back to dry ground. The car had to be pulled out and towed back to town, where they had to take the gasoline tank off and drain it to get the water out. Nowadays, the road is built up above the water line, and the road is paved. They don't have a water problem anymore.

Many times, when I was out playing, I would have a funny feeling that someone was following me. It would turn out to be my sister, Marjorie Anne. One day, I decided to climb a tree, and she was right behind me. She said that I fell out of the tree, but I don't know if I fell out or if she pushed me! All I know is I hit the ground hard. Everywhere I went and everything I got into, she was right behind me and was doing whatever I was doing.

When it rained hard, there would be a little stream flowing down the slight incline behind the house. I would make small paddle wheels (think mill wheels) and place them across the stream and watch the water turn the wheels.

When Daddy was principal of a school in Mt. Zion, we lived in the house that was connected to the school. It was an old house that didn't have any of the modern conveniences. West of the house, there was a pasture just covered in broomstraw. We went out there and gathered a bunch of the broomstraw, and Mother made herself a broom, which she used in the house and also in the yard. Generally, you had to make a bigger and stronger broom with which to sweep the yard.

Near where the broomstraw was located, there was a gully that had washed out. At the bottom of the gully was a lot of clay, which we would dig out, take home, and try to make marbles or anything else we wanted out of it.

Chapter 2

Fun with My Cousins and Friends

As a small boy, I stayed with my grandparents most of the time during the summer, as my father went to college in Hattiesburg. Since my cousins, Delmos and Hap (two of Uncle Milton's boys), lived only a short distance away, we played a lot together.

Uncle Skeet worked on an oil rig. When he came home, he would give all the boys a little money. Off to town we would go to buy firecrackers. When we got home, we would shoot them off. Sometimes, we would put the firecracker under a tin can to see how high the can would go. With all the firecrackers we shot, nobody ever got hurt.

We found out from a book how to make gunpowder, and off we set out to make some. After we made the gunpowder, we were never able to get it to explode. It would burn very fast and give off much smoke, but that was all it would do. We still found a use for it. First, we would find the entrance to a yellow jacket nest. Then, we would fill an iron pipe or a large segment of bamboo with the powder, and off to the yellow jacket nest we would go. We would light the gunpowder and stick the end of the pipe or bamboo into the entrance of their nest and then run. You did not stay around the entrance of the nest very long. The smoke from the gunpowder would kill the yellow jackets or knock them out for a while. We destroyed many yellow jacket nests this way.

Delmos and Hap lived on the next hill from my grandparents. A small creek ran between the two hills. As eight- and nine-year-old boys, we played a lot around this creek. We loved Tarzan and would find a vine to swing across the creek on. Also, we cut small poles about the size that they use at school for pole vaulting. With these poles, we would pole-vault across the creek. One or two water moccasins lived in the creek, so we had to be careful to go all the way across when we vaulted. Occasionally, one of us would make a miscalculation and fall in the water. How none of us got bitten is a mystery to me. In addition, a tree had fallen across the creek, and we used this tree to run and play on.

I would like to tell you a story of what you can find on this creek. One Sunday we went down the creek to where it crosses into the neighbor's pasture. A big tree had blown down near the creek, and a big hole had been left where the tree stood. There was water in the bottom of the hole, and lying around the water were some fifteen to twenty water moccasins, sunning themselves. We had our slingshots with us and shot rocks at them but could not do much damage. Some of the snakes slowly retreated back into holes around the water.

I saw a ghost one Sunday. My father was preaching at his home church (Pine Grove Baptist near Magee). The cemetery is next to the church. Delmos and I were playing outside until they started the service. I don't know why we were in the cemetery, but it was getting dark. We saw something white coming across the field toward us. There is a fence around the cemetery, but the white object kept coming until it was near the fence.

At this point, Delmos and I decided that it was time to get out of there and go to the church. I don't know how the white thing crossed the fence. I don't know if it climbed over or just came through the fence. We made a beeline for the church, which had a wing that extended out from the main sanctuary. We ran through this wing and sat down on the front seat. I don't remember whether the wing had a door that we went through, or if we climbed through a window. I kept looking for someone to come in the back door, but nobody ever did.

Delmos's older brother, Harold, saw an advertisement in a magazine for beer seeds. He sent off for some, and when they arrived, he and Delmos proceeded to follow the instructions and make some beer. They used fruit jars and put in all the ingredients that were called for. Not wanting their parents to know what they were up to, they took the jars with the mixture over to the edge of Grandpa's field and let it ferment.

After it had fermented several days, they decided to check it out and drink some of it. I asked them if it tasted like beer, and they said it tasted a little like it. The results were so disappointing that they never ordered any more beer seeds. I heard no more about them making beer.

When Daddy was preaching, I often went home on Sunday afternoon with one of the boys [from the church] to play. One boy and his brothers had a vine that they used to swing across a big ditch. I was going to be smart and act like Tarzan. The vine was hanging down in the middle of the ditch. I tried to jump and catch the vine and swing across the ditch. Bad mistake! I missed the vine and fell to the bottom of the ditch, knocking the wind out of myself and banging myself up good. I haven't tried that since.

One weekend I went home with another boy, and his brothers showed me how they climbed a pine tree, grabbed the top of it, and then slowly swung down to the ground. I thought I would try it, so I climbed up a small pine tree, grabbed the top, and swung out. The only problem was that the top of the pine tree broke, and down I came with a thud! You learn from all your mistakes. I won't try that again.

Since we did not have much money back then, we had to make things to play with. One Sunday, one of the boys showed me how to make a wooden truck from a two-by-four. We played with these toys, as other kids would have with bought toys. If there was something we wanted, we made it and had as much (or more) fun as kids who had the money to buy ready-made things.

We made our own kites to fly, our guns to play cowboys and Indians with, and wooden wagons, which we rode down hills in. One of the boys had made a wagon. Just west of his house were some hills that we would ride down. It was scary, because there were trees on both sides. If you did not go straight, then you could hit a tree.

We also made stilts to walk on, which has helped me today, as I lost both legs when I had bypass surgery, and I now walk on two artificial legs.

Chapter 3

At My Grandparents' House

One of my favorite times spent at my grandparents' was syrup-making time. I wasn't there all the time but would come home from school and watch them make syrup. They would cut all the sugar cane and move it to the place where they would make the syrup. They started by running cane through a machine that squeezed the juice out of the stalks. A mule went around the machine in a circle to do this. Every so often they would exchange the mule and put a different one in place.

    The juice was caught in a barrel. It was nice to get to drink some of the juice before sending it to the evaporator (or boiler pan). You had to be careful because of the yellow jackets and wasps that swarmed around the barrel, getting their drink too. A pipe ran from this barrel to the boiler pan, which had metal partitions in it with openings at alternate ends. Raw juice would run into one end of the evaporator, and several men would gradually work it along the pan until it reached the other end. A fire was going under the pan, and the water evaporated from the juice as it moved along. When the juice got to the other end, one person would let it out and fill the cans with syrup.

It was always great fun when Grandpa had a load of cotton to carry to the gin. Picking cotton is hard work. It is also hard on your fingers, because the burrs where the cotton is located prick your fingers to the raw. Thankfully, most farmers now have mechanical cotton pickers to do this work. After the cotton was picked, it was put in a shed to keep it dry.

When Grandpa had enough for a bale, he would load the wagon with the cotton, and off to the cotton gin we would go. The job of us boys was to get up on the cotton and pack it down so that they could get all the cotton on the wagon. When they headed to the gin in town, we boys rode on the back of the wagon. We made sure that we had our slingshots and plenty of small rocks for ammunition. When we passed certain houses, three or four dogs would come running out and bark at us. From the back of the wagon, we let the dogs have it with our slingshots. We never hit very many, but we slowed them down.

When we got to the gin, we pulled in under a big pipe that had a vacuum on it. This was where the cotton was unloaded. The cotton was sucked up through the pipe.

Grandpa would then pull the wagon out of the way, and someone else would pull in behind him. I still do not know how they knew when they had finished with Grandpa's cotton, and when they started on the other fellow's cotton. It was fun to go inside the gin and watch the cotton being ginned.

When it was over, out came a bale of cotton all baled up. Grandpa could sell it there or have it held a while, hoping that the price would go up.

If we were through in town, away we would go for home with us boys in the back of the wagon. The same dogs that barked at us when we were going to town were waiting for us on the way home.

Grandpa Padgett had a battery-operated radio that quit working. The only thing he liked to listen to on the radio was *Lum and Abner*. Well, I took the radio and looked in the back to see if all the tubes were working. One tube did not light up when the radio was turned on. I suggested that I could go to town and get a new tube to replace that one. Grandpa gave me the money, and I took the tube out of the radio.

I got a ride into town with Uncle Milton and found a store that sold radio supplies. The repairman checked the tube for me and discovered that it was defective. I asked the man if he had a new tube to replace it with. He did, so I paid for it and headed home.

Starting out walking, I got a ride with a man in a pickup truck. We came to the road where I needed to go, but the man was headed straight on. I started out walking again and walked several miles to my grandparents' house. I inserted the tube into the radio just in time for Grandpa to hear *Lum and Abner*. That really made him happy.

The older you get, the more you learn to do. Grandmother was to feed the visiting preacher for lunch. We did not go to a store and buy a chicken already dressed and ready to cook. Grandmother told me to go and get one of the chickens, wring its neck, and then chop off its head with the axe. I had never done this before. I had seen it done numerous times, but to actually do it was something else.

I caught the chicken and put my hand around its neck. I swung it around and around as I had seen my grandpa do. The chicken was still alive, so this time I swung it around more times than before. Finally, its neck broke.

Now it was time to chop off the chicken's head. I put its neck on a piece of wood and chopped the head off. Blood splattered everywhere. I gave the chicken to my grandmother, who had to scald it, pluck the feathers off, clean it, and cut it up before cooking it. My part in preparing lunch that day was a big learning experience.

When I was eight to ten years old and Grandmother or Grandpa needed something, it fell to me to go to the country store to buy it for them. The store was around three miles away by road, but if you went through the swamp and hit a different road, it was only about one and one-fourth miles. I was able to buy what they needed and a candy bar for myself. Sometimes I bought a drink or ice cream bar. This was a great treat to get something extra.

When I was around eleven years old, Grandpa taught me to plow. The easiest plowing that I did was with a sweep. You ran the plow down between two rows, and it threw the dirt both ways to lay by corn or whatever you were laying by.

Chapter 4

Easter Fun

Easter is the time for the Easter Bunny with a basket full of colored eggs, chocolate bunnies, and other good stuff. As a small boy, I will never forget looking forward to Easter morning to see what the Easter Bunny had left me. If you had a front porch, the Easter baskets would be all lined up on the porch with your name on your basket. If you did not have a porch, the baskets would be on the front steps.

Looking around really carefully, you might see a rabbit running to a bush for cover or slipping under the garden gate. We told Grandpa that we had seen the Easter Bunny, but he claimed that it was just a cottontail rabbit. You will never convince us children that it was only a plain old cottontail rabbit. What a happy time we had when we saw a rabbit—which we knew was the Easter Bunny—and when we found our baskets filled with eggs all colors of the rainbow, chocolate candy, and jelly beans.

After lunch it was time to have the eggs hidden in the yard, and we children would go and hunt them. When we thought that we had found all of the eggs, we would count them to make sure. Sometimes we were missing one or two, and a big hunt would start for them. The people who had hidden the eggs could not remember where they had hidden all of them. These eggs were finally considered lost.

Now, the dog had been shut up till the egg hunt was over. When the dog was turned loose, he went around smelling where the eggs had been hidden. If there were any eggs left, he was sure to find them. Late afternoon we saw the dog go behind the house with something in his mouth. We all went to see what he had, and, yes, it was one of the eggs that had been lost. It might be the same afternoon or several days later when Rover would find all of the lost eggs, unless they were hidden too high for him to reach.

When I was a small boy, most of the churches would have an Easter sunrise service and an Easter egg hunt during the afternoon. Everyone would bring eggs to be hidden.

One time, a group of smart-alecky boys brought some eggs that were not cooked. These were hidden with the boiled eggs. After the eggs were all found, then the people sat down and ate. You can imagine what happened when everyone broke the eggs. Some children got raw egg on their pretty Easter dresses, and some adults got raw egg on their Easter clothes. There were some very unhappy people at this egg hunt.

The pastor gathered everyone together and gave a very stern lecture about what had happened. Knowing who the culprits probably were, he said they should apologize to the entire congregation. He threatened that if it ever happened again, he would personally call each one to the front of the church to apologize.

I remember a funny story about an Easter egg hunt. While the eggs were being hidden in the yard, the children would have to stay inside the house. Outside, there were nests built for the hens to lay their eggs in. One small boy was peeping out the window and saw someone go to one of the nests and put something in it.

An old hen came to the nest to lay her egg. She did not look to see what was in the nest before she sat down. When she had completed her task, she looked to see what she had done. All she could see was a brightly colored egg. She set up such a racket that the old rooster came to see what she was squawking about. The rooster could not believe his eyes. He turned his head so that he could see the egg with his right eye and then looked at the egg with his left eye. He could not explain the colored egg, but he did tell the hen that she should stay away from colored corn from now on.

When all was ready, the children were allowed to go hunt for the eggs, and the young boy headed straight for the nest. He stuck his hand under the hen and grabbed the colored egg before the hen knew what was happening.

Finally, the old hen discovered that the colored egg was gone. Now the hen really set up a racket. This brought the old rooster back to see what was the matter this time. The hen said that the egg was stolen, and the rooster wanted to know who had stolen it. All the old hen could say was, "It was there, and now it is gone." The old rooster said, "Not only are you going to have to get off the colored corn, but you are going to have to lay off the sour mash!"

Easter Sunday is a special time when everyone looks forward to wearing their new Easter clothes. Also eagerly anticipated is the annual Easter Cantata by the church choir. Easter is a happy day for children. It is a lot of fun having the eggs hidden and then going to hunt them. The egg, of course, represents new life.

But let's look and see what Easter really means. Our Lord and Savior Jesus Christ went to the cross, where he suffered, bled, and died for our sins. Then he was put in a tomb behind a large rock, with Roman soldiers guarding the entrance to keep people from stealing his body. Easter is a day of remembering when Jesus Christ arose from the grave and, after forty days, went back to his Father in heaven. It is a day to remember what Jesus Christ did for us. Someone had to pay for our sins before we are able to face God. Jesus Christ went to the cross and took the sins of all mankind—past, present, and future—on himself as atonement to God.

Chapter 5

Family Stories

There are several stories that have been told down through the generations of my family. One of my kinfolk saw an advertisement in a magazine for a pair of divining rods that you could hunt buried treasure with. Well, they sent off and bought a pair of those rods.

One night they went out to a deserted house and used the rods to search for buried treasure. (Back then, people would bury their money in the ground. They would not put it in the bank, as they did not like or trust banks.) My kinfolk found a place where the rods indicated that there was something metal in the ground, so they started digging. One of the men hit his foot with the shovel and said a swear word. From that time on, there was no more indication of any metal from the rods. That spooked the men, and they headed home.

They also tell about going fishing on Cohay Creek one night. After setting out the hooks, they settled down in their camp.

After a while they started hearing a noise like rocks being thrown into the water. Getting up to investigate, they started walking along the creek bank, but the noise kept going along ahead of them.

Finally, they stopped and went back to their camp. The only thing that they could think of was that it was a ghost throwing rocks into the water, trying to get them to go home! That ended their fishing trip. They took up their hooks and went home.

Uncle Skeet told an interesting story that happened to him. There was a death in the house that was across from the country store. Everyone had gone to the funeral home, but Skeet was left at the house to greet any callers that might come by.

All of a sudden, he started hearing the most beautiful music that he had ever heard. He thought it was a radio and went through the house, looking for the source. Finding none, he looked outside to see if it was coming from a car radio. He could not find any place the music was coming from. After a little while, the music stopped just as suddenly as it had started. Your guess is as good as mine as to where the music was coming from.

Chapter 6

Fishing

I decided to go fishing one day, so I jumped on my bicycle and rode down to the bridge that was on the way to the church. I had a rod and reel, which I baited up and cast toward a bunch of willows. It did not take long before something hit my bait. I set the hook, and then I had fun trying to land the biggest bass that I ever caught. I finally got the bass close to the bank and was able to pick it up. Now I forgot about fishing. I put the fish in the bicycle basket and headed home. Somewhere there are pictures of me holding the fish.

☼

It was midsummer, probably around July 4, when someone suggested that we go fishing on Cohay Creek. It was decided that we would make a day of it and have a fish fry there too. Cohay Creek was north of my grandparents' house. You could use the main road for quite a ways, but then you turned off on a road where an old dummy line used to be. The road had four or five bridges that you had to go across to get to the creek. It was almost impossible to travel along this road, because the bridges had been built years ago and now were in really bad condition. Most of them had planks put across them so a car could cross (though barely).

Well, we packed two cars with people and other things, and away we went. We barely made it down the old roads and across the bridges to the place where we were going to fish. Everyone got a fishing pole and found a place to start fishing.

At lunchtime everyone came together, cleaned the fish, and had a big fish fry. My father was eating, while sitting with his back to a big tree. Someone shouted, "Don't move, Barney!" as a large snake came slithering down the tree beside him and onto the ground. The snake did not pay attention to anyone but headed out to the bushes nonstop. Apparently, the snake had gotten smoke in its eyes while in the tree and was getting out of there. Thankfully, it was just a chicken snake.

One day I got a fishing pole and found a place to fish. There was a dead tree that ran halfway across the creek. Standing at the water's edge, I cast my bait into the water close to the top of the dead tree. The cork was pulled under, and I pulled up, discovering that I had a perch on the end of my line. I raised the perch up in the air, but it was still flopping around trying to get off the line. It came off the hook and was falling back toward the water. I reached out with my left hand and caught the fish in midair. How I did this, I do not know. All I know is that I sure wanted that fish! That was one time in a million that this would have occurred. I have never done it again and probably never will.

The biggest snake I ever encountered was while fishing on Cohay Creek north of where we lived. You had to drive down an old logging road that was almost impossible to travel on. Delmos and I were going down the creek to find a better place to fish. I was in the lead, and I stepped up on a big tree that had blown down. I don't know what made me look down, but there, lying next to the tree, was the biggest water moccasin I have ever seen. He was at least the size of an eleven-year-old boy's thigh. The snake, having been discovered, started to move into a hole. Using our fishing poles, we started punching the snake until he was gone from sight. I think about what would have happened if I had stepped off the log onto this snake and been bitten by him. We were far away from a doctor or hospital for help.

Chapter 7

Animal Tales

I had a small dog named Trixie. One day she went with me down to the swamp. She found a snake and wound up getting bit by it. I thought Trixie was going to die. We made her a bed, from which she didn't move for almost a week. After seven days she started improving, and after two weeks, she was going her merry way. From then on, she became deadly to snakes. It seemed that she was now immune to the snake venom. Everywhere we went, Trixie was on the hunt for snakes. She hated them and killed quite a few. One day she killed a mother water moccasin and all the babies that were still inside of it.

Thanksgiving Day was a big day at my grandparents' house. Most of the kinfolk would try to be there. After lunch it was time to go hunting. Only the adults had guns, but all the younger boys would tag along. We hunted rabbits, squirrels, or sometimes quail.

One day we went hunting for rabbits. The dogs went with us, and one of the dogs found a skunk. He started barking at the skunk, and the skunk let him have it full force in the face. The dog fell backward and started whining like he had been shot. He started rubbing his face with his two front paws, trying to get the smell off. Then he lay down and rubbed his face in the grass. That ended the dog's hunting for the day. He headed for home. We gave him a bath when we got back from hunting, but it did not do much good. You talk about learning your lesson; the dog and everyone else had to live with that smell for over a week. He did not fool around with skunks anymore.

That day we did find a rabbit that started down a cotton row. The dogs were right on its heels, so it jumped over to the next row and headed back toward us. The dogs were really confused, and we were surprised to see the rabbit coming back our way. Someone finally shot it.

I was going through the woods to check on something for Grandpa, when I saw a big gray animal coming through the woods, going parallel to my track. It stopped and looked at me for several seconds, and I looked at it. I had never seen a wolf before, but I believe this was a wolf, from pictures that I have seen of wolves. I did not have a gun or even a stick to defend myself. After looking for a few seconds, it started to move on to where it was going, and I made a beeline for the house.

When we moved to Mt. Zion, Daddy bought a cow. As he was taking her home in a trailer, the car (along with the trailer) slid off the road. This caused the trailer to lean to the side. The cow fell sideways, broke the planks on the side of the trailer, and got out. We had watermelons and other stuff in the car and trailer. It was a mess. Luckily, the cow did not have any broken bones. We were about one and a half miles from home. How were we going to get the cow home? It was assigned to me to walk the cow home. I could imagine the cow not wanting to go straight home. I thought she would pull on the rope around her neck at every house we passed, but she surprised me in that she was no trouble. She went straight down the road, even with a few cars passing. I guess she was traumatized from the spill she had.

Let me tell you another cow story. Daddy bought a cow and calf from a man just north of Pine Grove Baptist Church. The calf got away from them when they were loading the mother into a pickup truck. The calf ran into the woods, and we tried to find it but failed. What were we going to do? We finally unloaded the cow and put her in a stall. She called all night for her calf. The calf knew the sound of its mother's voice and finally came home. Then we had to go back and get both of them.

One time my father let me go squirrel hunting with him and another man. The man had a squirrel dog, and his dog treed a squirrel. After looking to find the squirrel, my father shot it, and it fell to the ground. I ran to pick it up, but the squirrel was not completely dead. When I picked it up, it bit me on my thumb. Its teeth went all the way through the thumbnail and thumb. The squirrel did not like what had been done to it and took out its anger on my thumb. This was another learning experience: don't pick up a wounded squirrel until you know that it is dead.

When I was a teenager, my father bought me a rifle. One day, I went hunting for squirrels in the woods next to our house. I didn't see a squirrel but came upon a dead tree with a large hole in it. I proceeded to look in the hole, and when I did, I came face to face with a strange animal that growled at me. This shook me up, and I headed home. I decided that the animal could have the hole. It seemed that an opossum had taken up refuge there. I had never seen an opossum before. Now I know what one looks like and have seen them fight dogs.

Chapter 8

Foxworth, Mississippi

I was taught about the love of Jesus at an early age. When I was twelve years old, I realized that I was a sinner, was lost, and needed Christ as Savior. I struggled with this problem over a six-month period. One day after school, my father explained to me what it meant to accept Christ as Savior. At this point, I confessed my sins to Jesus and accepted Him as my Savior and Lord.

My father was pastor of Foxworth Baptist Church, and one of the members asked him to go fishing on the Pearl River.

They would set out lines, and every so often during the night, they would check to see if they had caught anything. When they said "fishing," I was all for it.

We drove to the member's house and followed him by a neighbor's house and through his pasture to a place where we would camp. We had to walk the rest of the distance to the river. As we walked the narrow road to the river, at one spot, the man said, "Stop!" He had seen a snake up ahead. Saying that the snake had been a nuisance for quite a while, he killed it with a gun.

We proceeded on to the dock where the boat was moored, and the three of us got into the boat and headed upstream. When we came to the place where the trotline was set, they asked me to get out of the boat and wait for them as they checked the line for fish. It was pitch black, and I was left standing on a narrow piece of land that slanted up about thirty degrees for about six feet. I had no light with me and was about three feet from the edge of the water, not knowing whether there was a snake or an alligator nearby. I couldn't see anything; it was so dark. After what seemed an eternity, they came back in the boat for me. They had caught one or two fish on the line and baited up the line again.

We went back to the camp, and there I stayed. I did not go with them when they checked the line again. I had had enough of that!

The same church member asked my father if he would like to help him kill a hog. My father agreed to help. Well, we got up early that morning and went to the church member's house. The pig was penned up and ready to be killed. They gave my father a rifle to shoot the pig with. My father took aim and fired. Apparently, the pig moved just as he fired. The shot did not kill the pig, and it broke out of the pen and headed for the swamp. We hunted for most of the morning before finding it. They finally shot the pig. Then they got a mule and pulled the carcass up to the house, where they put it in hot water to scald it so they could scrape all the hair off. After that, they hung it up and gutted it. Then the job of cutting it up began. We went home with several pieces of fresh meat that day.

On July 4, one of the members of the church invited us to go fishing at a creek north of his house. This was a little creek that ran into the Pearl River. A thunderstorm came up while we were fishing, so we headed for safety to the car. Daddy got to an old dead tree that was still standing. The stump of the tree was big and had broken off some fifteen feet above the ground. It was rotted out on the inside and had a hole in the front of it big enough for someone to climb into. He took the fish we had caught and took refuge in this old stump. The rest of us made it to the car.

We had just moved to Foxworth, when, for the first time, a girl asked me to go to a wiener roast. I was very timid and did not go with her. I think I went by myself.

There is another thing that occurred at Foxworth that is worth mentioning. One day we heard a large boom and, wondering what it was, went outside. Looking back over town, we saw smoke going up and heard the fire truck siren as they were going to the fire. I hopped on my bicycle and headed out to see what had happened. It seemed that a house had blown up. They had a leak on the gas line, and the house had filled up with gas. Somehow, there was a spark that set the gas on fire. There was one person in the house at the time. Thankfully, he was at or near the front door. He was not killed but had to be carried to the hospital. The house was damaged severely.

Chapter 9

My Teen Years

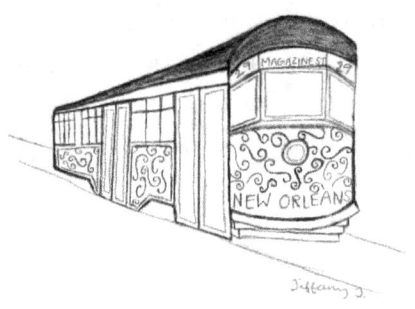

During the war (World War II), the boys my age would go around with our wagons and collect newspaper for the war drive. We would drop off the papers at a fire station and would earn a small sticker for a certain amount. It was funny what people would save. They would not throw any newspaper out but would throw them in a small room with magazines and other types of paper. We had to sort through all this to get to the newspaper. This was what we boys did for the war effort.

My cousin Delmos was one year ahead of me in school. When I was in the seventh grade, I was reading a book in the library and found out how to make an explosive using crystal iodine. (You had to take iodine crystals and soak them in a certain liquid, after which you would put the crystals out to dry. After it dried, any movement would cause it to explode.)

Delmos was in a science class where they had access to certain things. I asked him if he wanted to make some of the explosive. He said yes, but he did not have any of the crystal iodine. I went to the drug store in town. The druggist asked what I was going to do with the crystal iodine, and I told him that it was for an experiment in school. With no other questions, he sold me a small amount, and I gave the crystal iodine to Delmos. Well, he made the stuff, and after it dried, he put some of it in one of the books in the classroom. (I never found out where else he had put it.)

Three or four days later, the science teacher asked one of the girls to bring a certain book to the front of the room. The girl picked up the book and started to the front of the classroom. All of a sudden, the crystal iodine exploded! The book went straight up out of her hands, and she was so startled that all she could do was sit down. The teacher had a glass beaker in her hands, which she had a hard time trying to keep from dropping before she could set it down.

After things finally came to a stop, the teacher wanted to know who had shot off a firecracker in the room. Since nobody had, everyone said no. This ended the class for that period. The book had minor damage to its cover and front page. As far as I know, no one else knows what happened in that classroom that day. My cousin is now dead, and that leaves me as the only person who knows what happened. (But now you know also!)

A boy in school told me that he had made a crystal radio. He gave me a piece of the crystal and a diagram to follow. I proceeded to go home and scrounge up enough parts to build one. It would only tune to one station. We lived in an upstairs apartment, and I ran the antenna out a window to a chinaberry tree just outside. I was listening to my radio when they announced that President Franklin Roosevelt had died. I still have that radio and another one that my sister Mary Jean found in a kit just a few years ago.

My father went to Mississippi College in Clinton, Mississippi. People in the science department would discard glass tubing or other items that they used. I would go by every so often and look through the trash and find lengths of glass tubing, a glass funnel, or other objects that I thought I could use. After a while, I built up a store of objects that I could play with.

After my father finished his college work, we moved to New Orleans, where he went to school at the Baptist Bible Institute (BBI). This was the name of the Southern Baptist seminary on Washington Avenue. Since then, the name has been changed to the New Orleans Baptist Theological Seminary, and the seminary has been relocated to eastern New Orleans. The name change occurred soon after my father graduated, and the move sometime later.

Daddy found me a job at the BBI print shop. They needed someone to melt down the old linotype lead and pour it into a mold, so that they could use it again. This was right down my alley, as I had melted down scrap pieces of lead as well as old jar lids to make lead washers that we played with.

After a while, they trained me to do other things. I was moved to a small-job printing press, which was used to print small items, such as wedding invitations and school diplomas. I never got to use the cutting machine. They thought that it was too dangerous for a boy my age to use. While working there, I learned how to make a paper hat out of a large sheet of newspaper.

I had my first train ride while we lived in New Orleans. My father was preaching at a church in Mississippi, and I was going with him that weekend. We got on the train, and I had my window open. The train had a coal-burning engine. Well, when we started off, it did not take but a few seconds until I realized that the window had to come down. When they started up the engine, black smoke came back along the train. The smoke also had smut in it, and it drifted in the window onto my hands, arms, and clothes. It was another lesson I learned that day: don't leave your window up on a coal-burning train.

At that time in New Orleans, if you knew the routes of the streetcars, you could go almost anywhere for seven cents. You could get on one streetcar and ask for a transfer slip, which you could use to transfer to another streetcar, and to another if needed. One day I went swimming at Audubon Park, and my wallet was stolen. I found the wallet, but all of my money was gone. I found a transfer slip on the ground, which I used to get back home. Transferring two times in the process, I found myself about three blocks from home.

While I was in New Orleans, I learned what shrimp was. Another family invited us over one day. They had boiled some shrimp and invited us to come eat some. They came out with a large bowl of what looked like crawfish, which to me was fish bait, except that my fish bait looked better than what they brought out. Since I was company, I had to be polite and at least try it. The heads and tails were still on them, so I watched someone else take the head off and then the shell. The shrimp itself did not have much taste. I guess that's why some of the fish refuse to bite if you are using shrimp for bait. I asked where they bought it, and they told me some market. I said I could get mine free—all you had to do was go down to the creek with a piece of meat on a string, and the crawfish would grab hold of the meat, and you would pull them out. They laughed and explained that it wasn't crawfish. They told me to dip one into the sauce they had prepared and then try it. That greatly improved the taste, and I ate quite a few. I asked them how they prepared the sauce, because I wanted to make some at home to put on my fish bait.

I finished up my middle school work in New Orleans, and one year of high school. Then we moved back to good ole Mississippi. My father got a job as principal at Magee High School, and I got my high school diploma there.

I can remember one time when Uncle Skeet was home, he let us boys use his car to run around town. Since we were using the car, we bought him some gas to pay for what we had used. The price of gas was twenty-five cents a gallon then. A far cry from what it is now.

I did not have my driver's license very long, when my

father let me take the car one night to go to a football game. I picked up my buddy, and we went and had a good time at the game.

My buddy lived down a small road off the main one. There was only a very narrow single-lane road that led to his house, with ditches on each side of the road. As we started down the road, a rabbit ran out in front of me. I took my eyes off the road for a second, and the next thing I knew, we were in the ditch. We had to go and wake my buddy's brother and get him to get the tractor and come pull me out of the ditch.

When we got out of the ditch, I looked to see what it had done to the car. I sure hated to go home with the right side of the car scratched up. The next morning, I had to tell and show what I had done to the car. From this little accident, every time something else happened, they said it happened because I was "chasing rabbits."

The summer after I finished high school, I picked cotton for Uncle Milton. (I never could keep up with my uncle. He could always pick more cotton than I could.) I made one hundred dollars and got paid with a one-hundred-dollar bill! That was the first big money I ever made. This money went to help pay for my first year of college. That year I also planted five acres of corn on another man's land. Since I was in school when the corn was ready to be picked, we had to hire some men to pick it, and my half of it was sold to a nearby company that used a lot of corn.

Chapter 10

College

Well, we have come to the college years. I went to Mississippi College in Clinton, Mississippi, and worked in the library to help pay for my tuition. While I was there, we had a big ice storm that closed down the school. Everything was iced over, and limbs were broken off all the trees on campus. There wasn't much sleeping that night, as every time a limb would break, it sounded like a gun going off. During this storm one of the apartments on campus caught fire. All available boys rushed to the apartment to try to save the people's belongings, but there was not much they could do. The fire was finally put out, but there was not much left of the building. Daddy came to get me, and I went home until the college was able to open up again.

While I was in college, my other sister, Mary Jean Padgett, was born on October 15, 1949. After she grew up, she went to college and got her nursing degree. She then went on to get her master's degree in Birmingham, Alabama, and her doctor's degree at the University of Texas at Austin. After working several places, she became Dean of the School of Nursing at Mississippi College. She is the more ambitious one in the family.

My father was called to a church at Harperville, Mississippi. One of the church members was a building contractor, and I worked for him during two summers. One of the summers, we tore down the old school gym and started building a new gym, constructed out of cement blocks, in its place. Some two years after the gym was completed, a strong wind blew one end of the gym down. I guess there should have been more steel in the block wall.

One time, while I was working for this contractor, we went to Clinton and worked on a wooden boat dock. We stayed overnight at the camp and got in a little fishing before dark.

The Korean Conflict was going on during my college years. At that time, every young man had to register to be drafted into the armed services. I went to college summer and winter, since, as long as I was in school, my being drafted was deferred. I finished four years of college in three years, majoring in math with a minor in physics and education.

I was able to get a commission in the United States Air Force as a second lieutenant and was sent to Tallahassee, Florida, to meteorology school. (The funny thing is, I had never heard the word *meteorology* and didn't know what it meant until I was in Tallahassee. The recruiter simply told me I would be going to "weather school.") After I received my commission, I got another call from the air force to report to an air base to start pilot training. I had a hard time convincing them that I already had a commission in the air force and was being sent to weather school.

That Christmas in Tallahassee, school was out for several days. Since it was too far for them to go home, I invited two of the boys (Joe Smith and Dave Brown) to go home with me for Christmas. I did not have a car [at that time], but Dave had an old one, which he drove. It was cold, and his car heater did not work very well, but we made it home to Kosciusko, Mississippi. My mother was in the process of making a coconut cake, so she put us to work helping. She had one of the boys grate the coconut and the other do something else. She had something for each of us to do. I don't believe that Joe or Dave had ever eaten coconut cake before. We had a big time making the cake, and everyone thoroughly enjoyed it.

Chapter 11

Korea

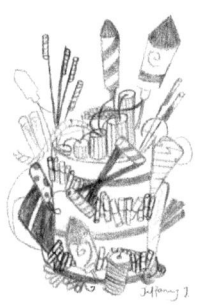

After completing meteorology school, I received my orders to go to California to catch a military plane and was given so many days to report. I headed out driving because I planned to have my car shipped to Guam, where I was supposed to be stationed.

I decided to go by Brownfield, Texas, and stop and say hello to Uncle Skeet, who was working on an oil rig there. When I passed through the Dallas-Fort Worth area, I ran into a dust storm. The visibility was down to about three car lengths. By the time I got to Brownfield, the visibility had improved. I found the motel where Skeet was staying but had to wait several hours for him to get off work and get back to the motel. We went to eat and talked and talked.

The next morning, Uncle Skeet headed to work, and I headed west. My car started acting up, and I thought that I was going to have to stop at a garage to see about it. By the time I found a garage open, the problem had fixed itself, so I kept going.

I went by the Grand Canyon and drove along the South Rim for a good distance. It is something to see. I would like to take a horse and ride down to the bottom and spend the night. I also stopped at Meteor Crater. When that meteor hit the earth, it sure dug an enormous hole.

From there I drove on to the air base at San Francisco, where I was told that I was being sent to South Korea instead of Guam. Instead of shipping my car, I went to a car dealership and arranged to trade my car in on a new one when I returned from Korea. It was against the law to bring a car into California to be sold, but since that had not been my intention, the dealership took the car as down payment on a new one. They sold the car to a boy who wrecked it on a mountain curve just a short time later.

Korea, here I come! From San Francisco, I flew to Japan on a government-chartered plane. We stopped in Hawaii and then at Wake Island for gas and something to eat. There was not much to see on Wake Island. The only thing I saw of interest there was the bow of a ship that had been sunk in World War II. All you could see was the bow; the remainder of the ship was under water.

We stopped in Japan and then took a military plane to Korea. While on our way to the plane that would take us to South Korea, we passed through an area of Tokyo that looked worse than a slum section. The houses appeared to be just little shacks. Tokyo has some very nice-looking sections, but this was not one of them. They had a market where you could go and argue over the price of an item with the person selling the goods. You could go from merchant to merchant and argue over the very same goods. Sometimes you could make a good deal on the article you wanted to buy. Taking off from Japan to fly to Korea, you have a good look at Mount Fuji, a volcano with snow on top of it. I would have liked to climb this mountain, if I had someone to climb it with me. The Japanese climb it all the time.

Now, on to Korea. I was stationed at Kunsan Air Force Base on the western side of South Korea, south of Seoul, about a third of the way up from the tip of the peninsula and located on the Yellow Sea just across from China. The only gold mine in South Korea is just east of Kunsan. I spent one year at the Kunsan Air Base. Most of the fighting had stopped about six months before I arrived, although before my arrival, someone on a small island off the end of the runway would shoot at the planes when they took off. I was one of the weather forecasters on the base. Our job was to give weather briefings to the pilots before their flights.

We had B-26s (small bombers) stationed on the base. The pilots told many stories about their flights north. One such tale was of the bombing of a North Korean train as it was coming out of a tunnel.

Every time a North Korean plane took off and headed toward our base, a warning siren would sound, and everyone would have to head for the bunkers made of huge stacks of sandbags. You could be in the middle of eating. It didn't matter. You had to go to the bunker. Strangely enough, I never had to head to the bunker while on duty.

One other thing we had to put up with was the firing of the antiaircraft gun. We only had one antiaircraft gun on base, but that was enough. It could be fired any time of the day or night. When we first arrived, it was startling to hear it being fired, as you didn't know if it was being fired at an enemy plane or not. As it turned out, they had to fire it every so often to make sure it was working and to train those who fired it.

Since there was a lull in the fighting, we were able to go into the village of Kunsan, and even go hunting. The air force furnished us shotguns and ammo, and it was there that I killed my first and only pheasant. The enlisted personnel who were hunting with me knew the cook, so they asked him to prepare it for all of the weather service personnel. I did get a couple of bites to see what it tasted like. Several of us came upon a rabbit, which we shot and gave to a South Korean family nearby.

For the Fourth of July, the commander of our base decided that we should have a big fireworks display. He took money (several thousand dollars) out of the base personnel fund and sent some people on a B-26 to Japan to buy fireworks, rockets, and so forth.

On the night of the Fourth, everyone on the base was gathered around where they were going to shoot the fireworks. The fire engine was there on standby. Every precaution was taken. They started shooting off the fireworks, but something happened. They let some sparks from the previous firing get into the ones they were going to fire. The whole stack of fireworks began going off! Everyone started to run for cover. I started out for a ditch, but when I got to it, it was full of water, so I had to continue on across the road to the other side of a building where others were taking cover. Have you ever tried to outrun a rocket? As I was running, a rocket came whizzing past me and kept on going. Others came whizzing past and kept on going. The fire truck personnel did not stand a chance. They had to take cover behind the fire truck. It only took a few minutes for all the fireworks to explode.

The next morning, men were out scouring the area for unexploded fireworks. We were very lucky that no one got hurt. The commander of the base was relieved of his command because of misuse of funds and was shipped out in a few days.

Things were very dull on base. A friend of mine (also a meteorologist) and I decided to take a walk on the shore of the Yellow Sea. As we walked that way, we went by a rice paddy on the edge of the base, which was really smelly since it was fertilized with human waste. Since it was low tide, we had plenty of muddy beach on which to walk. It was funny that there was neither a fishing boat nor any people in sight. We went up the beach as far as we wanted to, then turned around and were heading back, when all of a sudden, someone started firing at us. With bullets whizzing by on both sides, we hit the ground.

After the firing stopped, we got up and got out of there. Do you know what it is like to have bullets come close to you? You could hear them come sizzling through the air. What had happened was, we had come up behind the shooting range, where a high bank of earth was piled up to stop the bullets. It was a requirement that everyone take his turn on the shooting range every so often. A group of airmen were shooting, and they were not very accurate, as half of the bullets were going over the bank of earth.

It's time to leave Korea and go home. I was in Japan in December 1953 and was home by the next Christmas. On the way from Japan back to San Francisco, we stopped at Midway Island. It was really an experience watching the gooney birds there. They really put on a show. They would take off from the ground by running and flapping their wings until they got enough air speed. When they came in for a landing, they would make one or two somersaults before they stopped. In spite of their awkwardness in take-offs and landings, they are magnificent birds and can soar effortlessly for quite a long time.

Bernett's father,
Barney Evon Padgett

Bernett's mother,
Mary Ludie Gill Padgett

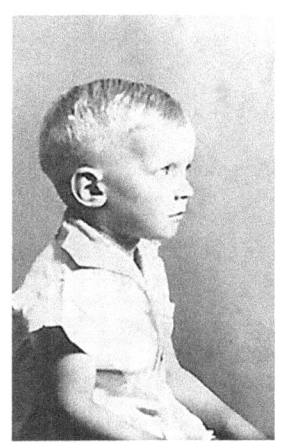

Lacy Bernett Padgett

Bernett's father with his siblings
Left to right: Rutha, Barney, Milton,
Rosie, Oredus, and Skeet

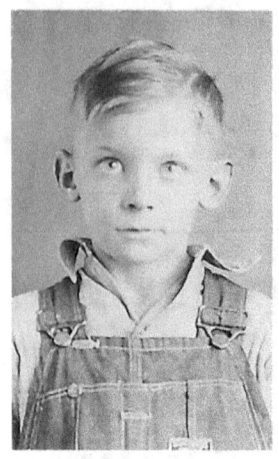

Elementary school photo of Bernett

Marjorie Anne and Bernett in Mt. Zion, Mississippi

Left to right: Bernett, Barney, Ludie, and Marjorie Anne. Mary Jean is in front.

Bernett with Mary Jean, on the occasion of his college graduation

First Lieutenant Bernett Padgett

Bernett at Kunsan Air Force Base

Checking the temperature

Respected grandfather (Harabeonim), Kunsan, Korea

Respected grandmother (Halmeonim) with child, Kunsan, Korea

This photograph was taken while Betty and Bernett were dating. They were at the Falls Creek Baptist Conference Center.

*Wedding Day!
March 14, 1956*

Betty and Bernett at the Gulf Coast on their honeymoon

Bernett is holding Eileen, and Betty is holding Margaret.

Bernett, hard at work at the weather office in Memphis

Counterclockwise from left: Bernett, Betty, John, Margaret, and Eileen

Counterclockwise from left: Bernett, Betty, and John

Bernett at the New Orleans Forecast Office in Slidell

Bernett and Betty at Ridgecrest Conference Center in North Carolina

Chapter 12

Ardmore

It was good to get back to the United States. Since I had made arrangements with the car dealer in San Francisco to get a new car when I came back, I went to the dealership and had Daddy wire me the additional money from my account that I needed to pay for the car. The dealer had made arrangements for me to pick up the car in Detroit. I flew to Detroit but did not know where the manufacturer was located. I asked a bus driver, and he said that he went past the building where I needed to go, so I hopped on board.

After picking up the car, I got directions back to the airport, so I could pick up my luggage. I drove down the expressway toward the airport and saw a sign reading

Airport. I turned off, but it was not the way to the airport. I had to make a loop and get back on the expressway. I came to the sign again and turned off. Wrong again. I did this three times before realizing that the sign was wrong. I finally got to the airport, got my luggage, and headed south toward Mississippi.

I drove on into the night until I realized that I had to stop and get gas. It was then I realized I was out of money. I had plenty in the bank, but none on me! I talked to the filling station manager and asked if I could give him a check. He really did not want to, but since I was in the air force, he let me use a check. I drove until I got sleepy and had to stop and rest. It was very cold, and I did not have a blanket with me. After a couple of hours, I started out again, and made it home to Kosciusko, Mississippi.

When I returned home, I was assigned to the 25th Weather Squadron at Ardmore Air Force Base in Ardmore, Oklahoma. I could not get over the dust storms we had there. One in particular stands out. We had a weather front move through with high winds of 60 mph and gusts above 70 mph. The personnel didn't have time to tie down all the planes, so a few of the planes were damaged. There was damage to a few buildings as well. A dust storm was associated with the strong winds. This is one time that it rained mud. We got only a few drops of rain, but when they fell through the dust, they were mud when they reached the ground. We also had several good snowstorms while I was at Ardmore.

First Baptist Church in Ardmore had lots of fellowships for the youth and the boys on the base. (Captain Woodrow

Rush and his wife, Eloise, worked with this group. My future wife and I became very close friends of theirs, and we have kept up with them all these years.) I met a young lady there, fell in love, and asked her to marry me. (Where is that dark haired lady? Now she has white hair!)

My wife, Betty, tells this story of how we met:

I had just come home from Oklahoma University (OU) for the summer. One of the girls from church was having a wiener roast at her home on Saturday night. I got all dressed up in a black sleeveless blouse, a white flared skirt, and a turquoise necklace. As I walked out the door that evening, I said, jokingly, "Well, if this doesn't do it, nothing will!" Mother and the kids all laughed, as I had never said anything like that before.

The boys on the base had been talking about some new girls in town. This young man walked up to me and introduced himself. He knew that I was going to OU and that I was majoring in pharmacology. We talked and had fun during the wiener roast, and then he asked if I would like to go to a movie. I said yes, so we drove by my house to leave my car and tell Mom where I was going. No one was home, so I left a note.

Unbeknownst to me, Aunt Mae and Uncle Calvin had picked Mom and the kids up and gone downtown to park on Main Street and watch the people go by. Suddenly, Aunt Mae said, "Why, there goes Betty!"

Neither of us can remember the name of the movie we saw that night, or even what it was about. That was the beginning of our courtship, and we dated all summer and through the fall. On New Year's Day, Bernett asked me to marry him.

We had picked out a date to be married in April. I found a furnished apartment with a living room, large bedroom, kitchen, and bath, and moved in.

Betty bought her wedding dress and made her headpiece and veil. Since we already had an apartment, we decided not to wait another month to get married. Betty and I made arrangements to go to Holly Bluff, Mississippi, where my parents were living, since of course, we wanted my dad to marry us. We were married on a Wednesday night (March 14, 1956). The ladies of the church decorated the altar, and the WMU (Woman's Missionary Union) bought our wedding cake for us. We went to Yazoo City to get our license, arrange for flowers, and pick up gifts for our attendants. Marjorie Anne was the bridesmaid, and Mary Jean was the flower girl. Aunt Rutha and Aunt Oredus came down for the wedding. Betty's family was not very happy that we eloped. Her brother said, "Now why did she have to go and do that?"

Since I had made arrangements for leave the next month, we waited until then for a honeymoon. We drove to New Orleans first, and I showed Betty the sights, such as Audubon Park and the French Quarter. We then drove on to the Gulf Coast to the Gulfport-Biloxi area where we had reservations at a little motel. I bought Betty a little sterling silver bracelet with a heart on it, and we had our initials engraved on the front and back. We enjoyed several days exploring the area. One day we went swimming in the Gulf of Mexico. I had an inner tube, on which I floated around in the water. It was a cloudy day, but I got the worst sunburn that I ever had. We had to go buy some Noxzema to put on it. We headed back to Ardmore, stopping on the way to see my parents in Holly Bluff.

One day I had gone downtown to buy something and came home with a little Singer sewing machine for Betty. A month and a half after we got married, I was scheduled to go to the town of North, South Carolina, to support parachute jumps for a month. I, along with a large group of other servicemen, boarded one of the planes to fly to South Carolina. Betty was watching us take off. We were roaring down the runway, when suddenly, the pilot put on the brakes. The fire trucks went screaming down the runway as a precaution. This was really scary for Betty, not knowing what was going on. The pilot had a problem with one of the engines, so he brought the plane back in to have the engine checked. Betty and I went to lunch at the cafeteria. After lunch I checked the status of my flight and was told that my plane was ready to try again. This time it got off the ground, and I was on my way.

While I was gone, Betty had plenty of time on her hands, so she went to town, bought patterns and some material, and put the little sewing machine to good use. She made a couple of blouses and a dress during that month.

Also, our church had a revival, with Angel Martinez preaching. Betty felt lonely, and Romans 8:28 helped her all the time I was gone. She put that verse to music, and the choir at First Baptist sang it one Sunday, with Betty and her two sisters singing the trio part. Betty told me that it was "our song."

We decided that we wanted a high-fidelity record player. I found out that I could buy the components and put one together myself. So, I bought a kit and built the amplifier. Then, I scrounged up some lumber and built a cabinet for our record player. I bought some oak and made a speaker cabinet. Our hi-fi player worked just great. I also bought our first record: *Swing Low* by the Percy Faith Orchestra. It still is a beautiful record.

My enlistment in the air force ended while I was at Ardmore. [However, Bernett did stay in the United States Air Force Reserve, and he had attained the rank of major by the time he left the reserve.] I joined the National Weather Service and was sent to the office in Memphis, Tennessee. We loaded all our possessions into a small trailer, and away we went. We got to Memphis, found an apartment, signed a lease, and went to spend the weekend with my parents in Holly Bluff. While there, we received a call from the Fort Worth office of the National Weather Service asking us to go to the New Orleans office instead. (A man in Memphis had left the Weather Service and wanted to get back in. He had a home there, and his wife was pregnant.) Fortunately, we were able to explain the situation to our new landlord, and he let us out of the lease. So, we moved to the New Orleans area and spent a couple of years there.

Chapter 13

New Orleans

More house hunting. We looked first in the area of Kenner, Louisiana, since the weather office was at the airport. We finally found one house for rent, drove to it, and were shocked at its appearance. The paint had all worn off, and the house was completely brown with age. In addition, the screens on the windows were very rusty.

We finally looked in the Metairie area and went to see a duplex on Pontalba Street. When we walked in the front door, we were greeted by the smell of fresh paint! What a relief, after the dilapidated houses we had seen. The duplex was a shotgun type and had a living room, kitchen with room for a dinette, two bedrooms, and a bath. There was a little shed at the back of the garage, which held a washer that we could use, so we didn't have to buy one. The owner and her adult son lived in the other half of the duplex. They agreed to put in a window air conditioner for us, since sometimes I had to sleep in the daytime. [Bernett worked shift work.]

I had saved most of my money while I was in Korea, so we were able to go downtown in New Orleans and buy our furniture. We bought a bed, a dresser, and a couch that made out into a bed, as well as a chair for the living room and a dinette set for the kitchen. Betty went to town and bought fabric for drapes and curtains, which she made with her trusty little sewing machine.

While in New Orleans, I took a television course that included building a TV set from a kit. I needed a table on which to work, so I asked the landlord if he had anything I could use. He loaned me a large round card table, as well as a chair. After completing the TV set, I turned it on to see if it worked. Voila! We had a good picture on it, but the vertical hold wasn't stable, so it had to be adjusted every so often to keep the picture steady.

When we moved from New Orleans, I sold the television to a friend for just the money I had in it. Even with the unstable picture, it was better than the one she already owned. We still have the card table and chair. We tried to return them, but the landlord said we should just keep them.

One morning I got up and headed out to work around seven o'clock in the morning. A little after eight o'clock, the weather office called Betty to ask if I was coming in to work. She was bewildered, since I had left the house an hour earlier. She made them promise to have me call home when

I got there. Then, she got on the phone with the highway patrol, told them I would be on Veterans Highway, and asked if there were any accidents out that way. They said, "No, but we think there is some fog there today."

I called home when I finally arrived at the office around nine o'clock, and did I have a tale to tell! Smoke was mixed in with the fog, and visibility was zero. I stopped the car every few yards, walked a little farther down the highway and back to the car, then drove a small distance. I practically walked to work that day. What normally took thirty minutes to drive had taken me over two hours!

While in the New Orleans area, we had a small tropical storm come through, and we went to the lakefront to see the water blowing over the seawall. We also had a light snow while there. We have pictures of both.

I wanted to go fishing, so I asked the boys at work for directions to a place. I drove over the Huey P. Long Bridge, followed their directions, and found the place they suggested. I did not think much of it. There was no place to fish unless you took a boat and went way back into the timber. Well, there was a pirogue tied up where I entered the bayou. (If you do not know what a pirogue is, let me tell you. It is a small boat made out of a log. When you sit down in it, you are almost at water level. It's really not big enough for two people.) I got in the boat and started rowing up the bayou. I looked around, and alligators were everywhere. They had their heads right at the top of the water. I began to wonder if this was such a good idea. I found a duck blind and tied the pirogue up and started fishing there. I only caught one fish. After a while, I decided that I had better quit and go home, if I could get through all the alligators. As I rowed back, there were alligators on both sides of the pirogue.

While in Metairie, we attended Canal Boulevard Baptist Church, which was not too far from where we lived. Bill and Pat Turner belonged to the same church, and they became very good friends of ours. The pastor was Bro. Ciocchio, an Italian who had read the Bible to disprove it and ended up becoming a Christian. He was raised Catholic and had brothers who were priests.

The WMU was having a large meeting at one of the downtown churches, and our pastor's wife was on the program committee. She found a little song that was supposed to be sung by someone in Japanese costume and asked Betty to sing it. They dressed Betty up in a Japanese costume and put her dark hair up in a bun with chopsticks in it, and she sang the song as she imagined a Japanese person would: kind of singsong and high pitched. After the program, Betty was changing into her regular clothes, when one of the ladies happened by and said, "Oh, honey, you didn't have to change clothes." She thought Betty was really Japanese!

Betty had her first miscarriage while there, and we had to wait a year before trying again. Finally, our first daughter, Eileen Rene, was born on March 14, 1958 (our second wedding anniversary!), at Ochsner Hospital in St. Charles Parish, Louisiana. Betty's mother came and stayed about a week to help out. My folks were living in New Orleans by that time, so it was nice to be able to visit back and forth with them.

Daddy was pastor of Valence Street Baptist Church, and my parents lived in the church parsonage. Before Eileen was born, we were driving down Magazine Street one day and saw a maple rocker on the sidewalk for sale: $10. We stopped and bought it. Betty rocked all our children in it.

One summer day, we decided to take Eileen outside and take some pictures of her. We sat her on the picnic table, and I was clicking away, taking a bunch of pictures. Imagine our chagrin when we had the pictures developed, and there was our precious daughter sitting right in front of a clothesline strung with men's undershirts! I was so focused on my daughter that I did not even see what was in the background.

Chapter 14

Huntsville

The summer of 1958, I was transferred to Huntsville, Alabama, to help open a new weather office there. While in Huntsville, we attended Southside Baptist Church. Huntsville was a nice place to live, but housing was in very short supply. The reason for this was that the government had brought a whole group of German rocket scientists, including Wernher von Braun, to the Huntsville area to work for the United States. (I briefed von Braun on the weather several times over the telephone.) We found nothing to rent, so we had to buy our first house. It had two bedrooms, a large living room, a large dining room, a tiny kitchen, a screened-in front porch, and a screened-in back porch. It also had a garage out back.

The screened-in front porch was an ideal place for Eileen to play when the weather was nice. One day someone knocked on the screen door, and when Betty answered it, a gentleman handed her our daughter! Betty was so flabbergasted she could only ask, "Where was she?"

"In the middle of the street," the man replied.

Neither of us realized that Eileen could open the screen door—let alone crawl down the concrete steps and toddle out into the street! Betty called me at work, and I picked up a latch for the screen door and put it on the minute I got home. We attached it so high that we knew Eileen could not reach it.

In Huntsville, there is an underground spring called Big Spring that comes out from under the hill in the downtown area. Also, there is a small mountain range just east of town. Several times when it was cold in the winter, we had rain at the weather station, but it was freezing rain on top of the mountains. Every spring, we could see the freeze line on the mountains.

One day we were eating, and things in the kitchen started to shake and rattle. It seemed that we'd had a small earthquake.

Aunt Ruthie (that's what we called Aunt Rutha) came to see us while we were in Huntsville, and we took a drive up Monte Sano (the mountain east of town). The clouds were very low that day, and suddenly, we were way above the clouds. Aunt Ruthie couldn't see over the edge of the road, and she said, "Oh, Bernett, let's go back down!"

Betty really wanted a piano. We finally found a big upright that was heavy as lead. We kept looking at the finish—it was so dark it was almost black. I decided I would refinish it. [Bernett took the whole piano apart (piece by piece) and carried it to the garage, where he stripped off all the old varnish and gave the wood a coat of linseed oil.] What a job that was! But it turned out to be mahogany and had a beautiful reddish tint. The tone of the piano was very good also, and Betty really enjoyed it. We had to sell it when we left Huntsville.

While in Huntsville, my wife and I had a rough experience. She was pregnant but began having problems in the fourth month. By the fifth month, the baby began to abort. We had no way of knowing if there was any heartbeat or movement of the baby, since an ultrasound was not yet available. The doctor said that Betty was losing too much blood, and that they must operate, even though they might be interrupting a pregnancy. A C-section was performed, and it was discovered that the baby had died early in the pregnancy, but it had turned into what they call a hydatidiform mole. The doctor said that it was very dangerous stuff, and he had to clean all of it out of her uterus. He showed it to me, and it looked like a bunch of grapes. We had to wait a year or more before trying again. When Betty got home from the hospital and was recuperating from the surgery, my mother came and stayed about a week.

While Betty was in the hospital, my boss's wife kept Eileen for me when I was at work. They owned a Great Dane, and she told Betty that one day she looked up, and Eileen was sitting on the dog's head!

One day my wife and I were home, and Betty was not feeling well. Suddenly, Eileen had a seizure. I was very upset, but Betty told me to check and see if Eileen had any temperature. I checked, and her fever was very high. That was the reason for the seizure. I called the doctor, and he told me what to do for her. After Eileen got well, she had no other problems.

One time my folks and a friend of theirs came to Huntsville, traveling in the friend's small Volkswagen. My father and his friend were going to the Southern Baptist Convention, over east in the mountains. Mother stayed with us while they were gone. I don't see how they made it, going up hills in the mountains in that small car. I thought they would have to get out and push when they were going uphill and then coast downhill, but they made it okay.

After spending a couple of years at Huntsville, I was transferred to the forecast office in Memphis, Tennessee. I hated to leave Huntsville, because it was such a nice place to live, but we sold our little house and said goodbye.

Chapter 15

Memphis

House hunting again. We went by Aunt Ruthie's in Jackson, Tennessee, and left Eileen with her, while we went on to Memphis to look for a place to live. We began looking in an area between Memphis and the Mississippi state line because it was close to the airport where the weather office was. After looking for two days, we finally settled on a brand-new home in a new subdivision. It had three bedrooms, a living room-dining room, kitchen, den with eating area, and two baths. I never will forget Grandpa Padgett's astonishment when we told him the house we were buying would cost $17,500! That was an unimaginable sum to him for a house. Seems pretty good in the current housing market.

Our second daughter, Margaret Ruth, was born on October 30, 1961, at Baptist Hospital in downtown Memphis. Aunt Ruthie had come to get Eileen, and she said that Eileen talked nonstop almost all the way back to Jackson. Aunt Ruthie brought her back home the day Betty was released from the hospital.

A few years later, Betty had her third miscarriage and had to have a D&C.

Since Aunt Ruthie's house was only about an hour and a half away, we went over to see her every chance we got. Margaret and Eileen would sleep in the twin beds, and one day, Betty heard lots of giggles coming from their room. Peeking in, she looked to see what they were doing. Eileen was reading an Uncle Wiggily story to Margaret, who thought it was hilarious.

Sometimes, Margaret would invite her friend, Susan Britt, to come with her to Aunt Ruthie's house, and they always had loads of fun.

One evening about dusk, we were driving toward Jackson, and suddenly, a figure jumped across the road right in front of us. It was either a bobcat or a panther. Betty and I both saw it, so we weren't imagining it.

Several things of interest happened while at the Memphis Weather Office. We had one observer who would go out and lie down on the roof to take the observation of the sky. One day the other personnel in the weather office decided they would play a trick on him (I was not involved in this). When he went out and lay down, they turned off all the lights in the office and locked the door. When the observer came back, he could not get in the office. It was like everyone had gone home. Finally, they turned the lights back on and let him back in. He was not happy about this.

One of the electronic technicians went with his friends to a bar not far from the office. He had too much to drink and started driving home. He drove his car up the guy wire on a power pole. Knowing that he would get a ticket if he called the police and told them what he had done, he told the police that his car had been stolen. This way, he would not get a ticket.

We had a big snowstorm (over twelve inches) one March 28. I was to go to work at five o'clock in the morning, so I got up and shoveled the snow off the driveway. I backed the car out and got into the street crossways, but I could not go either way because of the snow. I had to wake up my wife to come help me get the car back into the driveway. Then I called the office and told them that I was unable to get there.

Finally, that afternoon, someone came to get me in a truck. We had several snowstorms in Memphis, but this was the largest. This was the year of the garbage strike and the year that Martin Luther King Jr. was shot and killed there.

I can remember several ice storms in Memphis where the ice was on top of the snow. One storm occurred while I was working with some of the youth from the church. The group had made arrangements to go see a movie downtown. Well, it snowed some, and then freezing rain iced over the streets, which made the streets almost impassable. We loaded up the cars and headed downtown, just creeping along. At every red light, one or two of the boys would have to get out and give the car a shove to get it started moving again. Some of the hills were impassable.

As we were on our way home, we came to a hill on which several large trucks had gotten stuck about halfway up, so we turned off and went by the back roads. We made it fine but had to go a roundabout way to get back home.

When we first moved to Memphis, we joined, and were charter members of, Havenview Baptist Church. We met and became close friends with Warren and Annette Lowry while there. Warren was the Music Director at the church. [Bernett was ordained a deacon at Havenview Baptist Church. His father, Barney Padgett, preached his ordination sermon, and Warren Lowry sang.] After several years, an incident happened concerning the pastor, and we moved our membership to Broadway Baptist Church, where it remained until we left Memphis.

Bro. John Grayson Miller was pastor of Broadway, and his wife, Josephine (Jo), became one of Betty's dearest friends, along with Wilma Goode, Sara Crouch, and Mary Lynn Britt. One Sunday, after the morning worship service, Bro. Miller lay down on one of the front pews. His son was standing around talking to a friend, and when he checked on his father, he discovered that his father had suffered a heart attack and gone to be with Jesus. His wife was in the hospital at the time, having just undergone surgery. Bro. Miller had been pastor of Broadway for twenty years. It was a very sad time.

    I was on the building committee at Broadway Baptist Church. One year we had just completed building a new sanctuary, but there were still things that needed to be done before the dedication service and open house the next Sunday. During this time in Memphis, there was a curfew in place because of the garbage strike of 1968. Our work took us past the time for the curfew to start, and some of the people who were working on the church had to spend the night there.

    During the open house on Sunday, some of the nuns from the nearby Catholic school came to see the new building. Sara Crouch was showing them around, and they asked her if the chairs (in the choir loft) were for the rich people. She very graciously explained that the chairs were for the choir.

I worked with the RAs (Royal Ambassadors) at Broadway Baptist Church, and one year, David Mitchell and I took a group of the teenagers on a trip to Mammoth Cave in Kentucky. After setting up camp, the boys went exploring. David and I were sitting on a picnic table at the campsite, and everything was peaceful and quiet. Well, I looked down, and under the table, a skunk was marching along! He was probably looking for something to eat. You've never seen two men move so fast getting out of there.

    The next day we went on a tour of the cave, which was really interesting. We saw where people had explored the cave many years before and even places where they had died in the cave. Coming back out of the cave, we took a different route, with some of the boys singing a religious song as we came up to a place where we stopped to rest. Right up ahead, there were people waiting for their tour guide. The cave had a place inside where you could buy food, and tables and chairs were available. There was also an elevator that you could take to get back to the top. If you continued on the path, you would have quite a few steep steps to climb, and it was quite a few miles to walk. We went all the way!

Another time we took a group of RAs to Shiloh Military Park. First, we saw a movie in the welcome center, which explained what had happened there. It was really interesting. We saw the stream that they said was red with blood after the battle. According to oral family tradition, my great-great-grandfather, Elijah Lacy, was killed at Shiloh, and his grave has never been found. Many there were buried in a common grave.

We went with the RAs to several more places, one of which was to a lake south of Memphis for a camping trip. The Memphis Baptist Association called and asked if they could photograph some of the boys on the trip. Our pictures were put in an RA brochure that was distributed nationally.

Another interesting thing happened in Memphis. We had a pilot of a commercial plane call in, saying that he had one landing gear that failed to lock in the down position. While he was burning off some of his fuel, they foamed the east-west runway. The weather office was located just off the west end of this runway, so we had ringside seats to this mishap. When the plane came in to land, the pilot made a very good landing. It looked like his landing gear was fine, but as soon as weight was put on the gear, it failed. The left wing hit the ground, and the plane went sliding down the runway before sliding off onto the grass and stopping. They were very lucky to have only minor injuries on board.

We decided to add a large room onto the back of our house. It would have large windows facing the east and north, which would be an ideal spot for plants. (Betty really loves flowers.) A good friend of mine, Don Franklin, was also a good carpenter, so I hired him to help me (or rather, I helped him!) build the room. I did most of the finishing on the inside after we got the frame up, the roof on, and the windows in. We hired someone to do the brickwork.

Then I laid the oak flooring. It took me all of one day, and I burned my hand on the hot tar I had to use to cement the boards on which the flooring was placed. I rented a machine to put in the flooring, but it still was backbreaking work to swing that sledgehammer for one whole day to make the boards fit tight so they could be nailed.

We really enjoyed our new room, and eventually walled off one end of it to form another bedroom. Looking out of the east window, we could see and hear the planes above the trees as they gained altitude. Over time, we got so accustomed to the planes that we didn't even notice the sound of their engines.

Our only son, John Edward, was born on August 23, 1969, at Baptist Hospital. Before John was born, Betty and I were lying in bed one night, talking about how old we would be when the baby graduated from high school. I said, "We're too old for such foolishness."

"It's too late now!" Betty laughingly replied.

My mother came up and stayed with us for a while as Betty was recuperating from the C-section.

I went fishing with my friends from the office quite a few times. In the spring of the year, the striped bass would run in bunches. We would go to the Tennessee River below Pickwick Dam to go fishing. One day, we struck it lucky and found a place where they were really biting. We stayed in one place and caught over one hundred bass.

There was a store across the river where we could buy cokes and snacks. We stopped fishing around noon and went to the store to buy lunch. One of the guys thought he was a lady's man. He was flirting with a young woman in the store when her boyfriend came in. The boyfriend had a gun with him, and our guy decided he'd better get out of there. After lunch, we went back across the river and finished fishing.

Chapter 16

Picayune

I had always said that if the New Orleans Weather Office ever moved to Slidell, Louisiana, and an opening came up, I would apply for it. Well, in 1979 that office finally prepared to move to Slidell, and I was transferred there as one of the lead forecasters. I had to report to work in February, so I stayed in a motel in Slidell while looking for a house. We could not sell our Memphis home until June, when Margaret graduated from SBEC (Southern Baptist Educational Center). I did not want to live in New Orleans or Slidell, because of the proximity to the Gulf of Mexico (or, more accurately, the Mississippi Sound).

Betty and I looked in the area of Picayune, Mississippi, and had just about decided on some land to purchase. We spent the night in Hattiesburg, and it poured down rain all night long. When we went back to Picayune the next morning, the lot was under water! Needless to say, we did not purchase that land.

We finally found a new house just outside of the Picayune city limits, and I moved into it. I would go to Memphis on my days off and bring back a load of things in the trailer that we had purchased. We had a rollaway bed, which I took to the new house to sleep on. Every time I went to Memphis, I came back with another trailer loaded down. Didn't know we had so much junk!

While the forecast office was in the process of moving, I worked at their office in the post office building in downtown New Orleans for a few weeks before the move.

The workers there told me how it was when a New Orleans sniper was on top of the building next door. They even showed me the window he shot the bullet through, apparently at one of the workers.

Well, the big move came. We made a forecast and transmitted it, then jumped in our cars and drove some twenty miles to Slidell, made the next forecast, and transmitted it there. (The technician had already moved some of the equipment to the new office ahead of the move.)

Over time we upgraded our equipment to AFOS (Automation of Field Operations and Services). They have since been upgrading to just personal computers. The New Orleans Forecast Office now has a brand-new building just south of the Slidell airport. Also, we got a new radar system (NEXRAD). They shut down the small local office at the airport in New Orleans and let the FAA do the weather briefing there. It is hard to think what they will have in the future. Maybe they will have an office with robots doing the work and making the forecasts!

When I first went to the New Orleans Forecast Office, I started out as one of the lead forecasters on shift work. I made forecasts for the planes and for the Gulf of Mexico. Shortly after the move to Slidell, I was selected, along with the MIC (Meteorologist in Charge) and another forecaster, to go to Monterey, California, to attend a Marine Forecast School. We three flew to San Francisco, and then rented a car to drive south to Monterey. This drive was an experience, as we drove through some fields where they had vegetables planted.

When we got to Monterey, we had to stay in a motel for a few days before we were moved into other quarters. As we had a car, we could drive along the coast during the weekend. We were given tickets to drive along the seventeen-mile circle around the ocean where Pebble Beach Golf Course is located. The homes of some famous people are there also. If you don't have a ticket, you have to pay at the gate. The school got tickets for whoever wanted to go see the area. We drove a long way down the shoreline, and one day we ate at the Fisherman's Wharf in Monterey. There were sea lions everywhere around the wharf.

Roseland Park Baptist Church in Picayune (of which we are members) is very mission minded. When Bro. Gene Smith was pastor, the church planned a mission trip to Ohio to help a struggling church there and to minister in another area, doing construction work. Betty, our son, John, and I were assigned to the church, where we went door to door, witnessing to people and inviting them to the worship services in the evening. The youth helped with a Backyard Bible Club, and Dana Rose and Alethea Walker were in charge of the crafts.

On the way home from the mission trip, my family drove up into Canada and over to Niagara Falls, which was really exciting. We dressed up in rain gear and went down to several observation decks, where we could get a closer look at the falls, and even go behind them. Coming home, we went through New York, Pennsylvania, West Virginia, and Tennessee, and then home to Mississippi.

Some years later, the church planned a mission trip to Belarus. Everything was all set until Belarus closed the door for visitors. Then the trip changed, and we went instead to Poland. We flew into Warsaw and were met by the pastor of the church where we were to stay. We stopped at the seminary in Warsaw, where I purchased a Polish hymnbook for Betty. (When we got home, we had the church pianist play from that hymnal any hymn number that people called out. Most of the songs were very familiar to us.) Then, we drove on to Bialystok, Poland. We were close to the border with Belarus, and one day we drove a roundabout way and walked across the border. We wanted to say that we had gone to Belarus.

Poland is quite a country. Out in the rural areas, things were still quite backward. They had not caught up with the times, but they are making progress. We split up on Sunday. Pat Weaver and I went to one town to speak at the local church, and Dan Young went to a different town to speak at that church. Our pastor, John Brock, spoke at the church in the town where we were staying. At night we stayed at a nursing home, and I spoke there and gave out the little ribbon crosses that Betty had made for me as a witnessing tool.

One night, just before we left to come home, the vehicle belonging to the church was stolen. Another church member had to use his car to transport us back to Warsaw for the flight home. We all bought big fur hats and wore them when we arrived home.

Another mission trip that the church made was to Peru. Several members from Roseland Park Baptist Church, including one dentist from the church and another from Slidell, went on this trip. We flew down to Lima, where we were supposed to take another plane to Cajamarca. The tickets got messed up, and six of us had to wait and take the bus late that night. Martha and Marvin Mercado stayed with us, as they spoke Spanish.

During the day one of the missionaries in Lima gave us a walking tour through the city's downtown area. We saw the underground tunnels, the Chinatown section, and other interesting things. She then took us to the bus station where we boarded a bus that would take us to Cajamarca. It would be an all-night trip; we would arrive there the next morning. They made an announcement before we left (which Martha translated) that the restroom was for liquid only. If you had to do the other, let the driver know, and they would stop the bus and let you off, where you could do your business. The bus stopped at several towns to leave freight or take on passengers. After leaving the flat land along the coast, the trip was uphill, downhill, and around curves, as we went from sea level to around 8,920 feet at Cajamarca.

From there, we used the missionaries' cars to go on up to Yanacancha, another village which was about 11,000 feet in elevation. The people had heard that we were coming, and they had come from all the surrounding areas to have their teeth fixed or pulled. Marvin and Martha ministered to the people who were waiting in line to see the nurse or the dentist.

The next day, four of us (Robert Smith, Greg Koepp, Melvin Kuhlman, and I) went back to Cajamarca to work, building small chairs for the school at Yanacancha. Missionary Larry Johnson has a school in Cajamarca, as well as a woodworking shop. He also had the timber that we needed to build the chairs. A native of Cajamarca was in charge of the workshop, and he showed us around, stayed with us, and helped us while we worked. Greg knew how to run the saw and was able to saw the timber into the boards that we needed. After the chairs were made, we loaded them up and took them to the school in Yanacancha.

Then it was time for us to go home. When we got back to Lima, we did a little shopping before flying back home. I bought some marble figurines, a wall hanging, and a silver and turquoise necklace for Betty.

Part Two

Betty's Memories

Chapter 17

Weatherman

Bernett was always conscientious and hardworking, and really enjoyed his job as a weatherman. Once, when he was stationed at Ardmore Air Force Base, he realized that very strong straight-line winds (one hundred miles per hour) were coming through the area pretty quickly. He alerted the base, and they had time to tie down some of the planes. Since he recognized the danger before the forecasters did at Tinker Air Force Base in Oklahoma City, there were fewer planes damaged in Ardmore than in Oklahoma City.

However, he wasn't always correct in his forecasts. One time in Memphis (before the era of satellites and radar), when Bernett was at work, we were talking on the phone, and I asked him, "When is it going to rain?"

"It's not going to rain," he replied.

"Yes, it is," I said. "My big toe hurts."

Sure enough, it rained that day.

Through the years, Bernett had to endure many jokes about the incorrect forecasts that meteorologists sometimes make, but he just laughed them off, good naturedly.

For most of his career, Bernett worked three different shifts (morning, afternoon, and night), with it changing from week to week. It was hard on the whole family, because each week they would have to get used to a new schedule. Sometimes, when severe weather was threatening, he would have to stay over at the office until the storm was over. While he was working at the Slidell office, Bernett finally became Deputy Meteorologist in Charge, which meant he was on day shift all the time. This was a lot easier for everyone.

As a part of his job, Bernett kept up to date on all the latest technology. In Memphis, he took night classes in several computer programming languages. Many years later, the weather service in Slidell decided to update one of their computer programs from Basic to Fortran. Margaret, who was majoring in computer science, helped her dad convert the program.

After Bernett retired from the National Weather Service, he continued his interest in the weather. In his backyard, Bernett had an official weather bureau rain gauge, which he checked regularly, recording the rainfall amount in a notebook. He always watched the weather forecasts on

TV. From listening to Bernett talk about it, I learned how to watch the radar and have a pretty good idea when the rain would arrive in our area.

Someone from the National Weather Service told Bernett this funny story of something that happened after he retired. The secretary was checking the phone bill to make sure there were no unauthorized calls. (Long-distance calls were still itemized at that time.) The new Meteorologist in Charge asked what she was doing.

"I'm checking the phone bill," she said.

"Well, just pay it," he said.

"Bernett Padgett trained me, and *I check the phone bill,*" she replied.

With Bernett's retirement, we had more time to spend together. We purchased an RV and made quite a few trips to Oklahoma to see my family. Since both of us really loved the mountains, we also traveled to the Smoky Mountains several times, thoroughly enjoying God's majestic handiwork.

Chapter 18

His Faith

Faith in Jesus Christ was a central part of our lives. As a family, we worshiped God regularly. Bernett's father was a Baptist preacher. In addition, my grandfather and three of my uncles were Baptist preachers.

Both of us have always loved music. Many times, at home or when we were driving, Bernett would often start whistling hymns and then singing them. I would join him, singing the alto part.

In Memphis we bought a really nice piano, which I thoroughly enjoyed playing. All three of our children took piano lessons. Eileen decided to take organ lessons also, so we purchased an organ. Both she and I got a lot of pleasure out of playing it. When John was in sixth grade, he started taking trumpet lessons and learned to play quite well.

Bernett always supported me in my musical endeavors. I have written several anthems, the majority of which are based on scripture. One of them, "The Earth is the Lord's," was one of thirteen songs selected to be played in Tennessee on public broadcasting during the United States Bicentennial celebration. A copy of the song is in a time capsule somewhere in New York.

Bernett was always active in our local church, serving as a deacon and on various committees. In Memphis, he was on the building committee for the new sanctuary at Broadway Baptist Church. When the committee wanted to change something in the blueprints, they would send Bernett to talk with the architect, who *did not like* changes at all. Bernett seemed to be the only one who was able to convince the architect to agree to the changes without too much problem.

In Picayune, Roseland Park Baptist Church has a senior group called the BALL (Be Active, Live Longer) Club. The group sometimes went on short trips to see points of interest in the area and longer ones that required overnight stays. Many times, Bernett drove one of the vans for those trips.

Bernett wrote the following testimony of his faith.

This I Believe

Over two thousand years ago, God told His only Son that men on earth could not keep the laws that He had given. It was time to send Him to earth to die on an old rugged cross as a sacrifice for all man's sins. Jesus went to earth as His Father commanded. By being born to a virgin named Mary in Bethlehem, He took on the flesh of man.

He grew up in Nazareth and started His ministry when He was around thirty years old. He called twelve men to be His disciples, one of whom later betrayed Him. People came from all over to hear Him teach. During His time on earth, He healed the sick, caused the blind to see and the lame to walk, fed five thousand with a boy's lunch, raised a man from the dead, and did many other miracles.

The religious leaders were jealous of His popularity, so they plotted to have Him put to death. Many people believe that the Jewish people put Him to death, but Jesus went to the cross freely, where He suffered, bled, and died for the past, present, and future sins of all mankind. He could have called ten thousand angels to His aid had He so chosen. His body was placed in a tomb behind a large rock with Roman soldiers guarding it.

The officials thought that was the end of Him, but on the third day, Jesus arose from the dead. HALLELUJAH! HE AROSE! He went back to heaven, where He now sits at His Father's right hand, making intercession for us.

Ephesians 2:8–9 states: "For by grace are ye saved through faith; and that not of yourselves: it is the gift of God: not of works, lest any man should boast."

Just because Jesus died on the cross for your sins does not mean that you will automatically go to heaven. You must first:

1. Admit that you are a sinner and need Jesus.
2. Believe that Jesus is God's Son who died and rose from the grave to atone for your sins.

3. Ask Jesus to forgive your sins, save your soul, and begin His loving relationship with you.
4. Invite Him to come into your heart and be the Lord of your life.

After doing this, you need to thank Jesus for dying on the cross as an atonement for your sins and strive to live for Him from now on.

When a person accepts Jesus Christ as Savior, he will start a new life and leave the old life behind. If any person is reading this and has not accepted Jesus Christ as Lord and Savior, then this is the day you need to make a decision for Him. Don't put it off and say that you will do it next week or next month. By not accepting Jesus as your Savior, you have just rejected Him. You don't know when you will die. You could die of a heart attack or in a car wreck this very day. This could be the last chance you will have to accept Jesus Christ as Lord and Savior.

Chapter 19

Mediterranean Trip

We had always wanted to go on a cruise but had never had the time or the money. One day, we got a flyer in the mail from a Christian cruise company. I glanced at the information about the different tours with Dr. Adrian Rogers and his wife, Joyce. (Adrian Rogers was a former pastor of Bellevue Baptist Church in Memphis, Tennessee.) One went to the Mediterranean, and I thought, *That would be a really nice cruise.* But I didn't know how Bernett felt about it, so I handed the flyer to him and casually said, "You might want to look at this."

After glancing through it, he said, "That Mediterranean one looks interesting."

Yaaaay! I said to myself.

So, in June 1996, we took what we considered to be our fortieth wedding anniversary cruise. We flew out of JFK, had a fuel stop in Rome, and then flew on to Athens, where we checked into our hotel.

The next morning, the tour buses took our group for a day trip to Corinth. We saw the Corinth Canal, which connects the Aegean and Ionian Seas. Bernett said it was a mighty big ditch. Everywhere we went, the tour guides told us the biblical significance of each spot. We walked among the ruins in Corinth and saw the Temple of Apollo and the bema (the judgment seat), which Paul was brought before in Acts 18:12-17. Corinth is famous for its pottery, so I bought a vase at a potter's. Next, we boarded the buses and went to Mycenae. We saw the acropolis with the temple ruins, the Lion Gate, and the Tomb of Agamemnon (a.k.a. Treasury of Atreus).

Our final stop, before heading back to Athens, was the outdoor theater at Epidaurus, which has fantastic acoustics. One could stand in the center of the stage and be heard throughout the entire theater. Joyce Rogers sang "What a Mighty God We Serve," and another young lady sang "How Great Thou Art." Bernett went all the way to the top seats and filmed with his video camera from there.

The next day we toured Athens by bus, driving by the Olympic Stadium, the Old Royal Palace, Constitution Square (Syntagma Square), St. Paul's Anglican Church, and the Temple of Olympian Zeus. We got out at the Olympic Stadium and walked around. Our next stop was the base of the Acropolis. As we climbed toward the Parthenon, we came to Mars Hill (Areopagus), where Paul preached (see Acts 17:16-33). They advised everyone that the marble steps were worn and very slick. I decided not to try it, but Bernett climbed to the top and waved at me. The Parthenon, which at that time was being restored, was still very impressive. After the tour, we boarded our ship, the *Aegean Dolphin*.

The next day we sailed to the island of Rhodes. We toured a Byzantine church, which contained many religious icons, beautiful carvings, and small stones laid in very ornate patterns to form the floor.

From Rhodes, we sailed to Egypt. Landing in Alexandria, we boarded our tour buses, which were escorted by police everywhere we went. Whenever we crossed into a new district (checkpoint), another police escort would take over.

At Giza, we saw the Great Sphinx and the pyramids. Everyone gazed in wonder, trying to comprehend how hard they were to build. A single block was much taller than my husband. Many of us were pinching ourselves, as we could hardly believe we were on the other side of the world. The Egyptian Museum was fascinating; with so much to see, one could not take it all in. Fortunately, we were able to see the King Tut exhibit there, which we had missed when it was in America.

On our way out of Egypt, we drove through Old Cairo and Heliopolis and stopped to tour a Coptic church. Inside a glass case in the front of the church was a map of the holy family's journey into Egypt. The tour guide told us that the Egyptian people were very proud that they had helped save Jesus' life. In a remote area on our way to Port Said (the ship had sailed on ahead to meet us there), we saw a huge *Avon* sign. It seemed strange to see this touch of home so far away. Boarding the ship, we cruised overnight to Israel.

Our ship docked at Ashdod (a military port in Israel), and we were warned not to take pictures of anything there. Heading to Jerusalem, our tour bus stopped first at the Mount of Olives, where Dr. Rogers gave a devotional.

Afterward we went to the Wailing Wall and had lunch at a kibbutz. Our next stop was Bethlehem and the Church of the Nativity. After some shopping, we returned to Jerusalem.

The Garden Tomb was the most touching site in Jerusalem. As we turned to leave the tomb, we saw on the door, in bold letters, the words "HE IS NOT HERE—FOR HE IS RISEN." After we returned to the bus, our group burst out in song with "He is Lord" and "In the Garden." When we finished singing, the tour guide exclaimed, "Beautiful!"

We spent the next day on board ship, traveling to the port of Kusadasi, Turkey. Arriving the next morning, we took a bus to Ephesus, where we toured the purported home where the Apostle John took care of Mary, Jesus's mother. Next, we walked among the extensive ruins at Ephesus, which are spectacular. These were the most well-preserved ruins that we saw.

On the way back to Athens, we stopped at the island of Patmos and toured the Monastery of St. John, where they have a fifth-century copy of the Gospel of Mark. In the Cave of the Apocalypse, where John had the vision of Revelation, you can see impressions from his hands and knees.

After we arrived back in Athens, we had two free days, so we walked around and explored old Athens and did some shopping.

On our return flight, we had a fuel stop in Paris. As we were waiting, a little girl exclaimed, "Look, Mom. Rabbits!" Sure enough, there were rabbits running all about the runways. We arrived home tired but really glad that we had gone. It was a trip of a lifetime!

Chapter 20

Just Routine

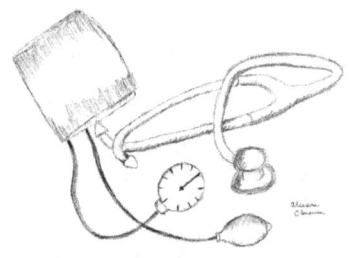

In January 2001, when Bernett was seventy years old, he noticed that he was having some shortness of breath when he walked a short distance to get the mail or to take out the trash. We consulted with a cardiologist, who scheduled an angiogram in February. The test showed that Bernett had five blockages in his heart, and bypass surgery was scheduled for February 20.

It would just be routine bypass surgery. The surgeon would go in, bypass my husband's clogged arteries, and everything would be fine again. But the surgery wasn't scheduled until the next Tuesday; we had almost a week to wait! It seemed like an eternity—that week. We savored every moment, holding each other close every night, and holding hands almost all Monday night.

Everything went well during surgery, and the recovery period began. Bernett seemed to be doing well. Each day brought more strength and color to his cheeks. But there was this nagging feeling that his recovery was not going as fast as the nurses said it should.

Despite my misgivings, we went home on the Monday after the surgery. Bernett's strength still did not return, and Wednesday he felt much worse. Staying in bed, he struggled all day with pain in the abdomen. I consulted several doctors by phone, and they told me to give him some antigas medication. Since the pain was not in his chest, there seemed to be no cause for alarm.

By evening, our only recourse was the local emergency room. The doctor and nurses there were all business, and they swiftly did an EKG. Calling me aside, the doctor said that my husband was having a heart attack, and they must transfer him to Northshore Regional Medical Center (in Slidell, Louisiana, about twenty minutes away) at once.

Leaving him only long enough to call my daughters (who lived nearby) and our pastor, I then watched as the nurses gave Bernett an aspirin to chew, inserted an IV, and made him as comfortable as possible.

After Eileen and Margaret arrived at the hospital, they called John and Bernett's two sisters, Marjorie Anne and Mary Jean.

When the ambulance arrived, the nurse said, "We don't have the paperwork ready to send with him."

"We'll fax it to them," the doctor shot back. "He can't wait for the paperwork. He must get there as soon as possible."

I rode in the front of the ambulance. We didn't travel less than eighty-nine miles per hour and were at Northshore before midnight. (Eileen and Margaret followed the ambulance to Slidell. A few hours later, John and my husband's two sisters arrived.) An angiogram was done, and it was confirmed that there were more blockages. The surgeon was called, and once again, bypass surgery was performed.

After the surgery, the first question out of the surgeon's mouth was, "Is he allergic to Heparin?"

"We don't know," we replied.

The surgeon said they cut open the first bypass, and it was full of clots. Apparently, my husband was allergic to Heparin—this drug that is the preferred drug of choice for every bypass surgery done today. I was later told that there was a special medication, Refludan, which would be given in this case, if they could find some. They checked with the hospital pharmacy, which, thankfully, already had some on hand, as another patient had required it a short time before!

Bernett's lungs filled with fluid, his kidneys started failing, and his platelets dropped drastically. He breathed with the aid of a ventilator. Eventually, a tracheostomy was performed, and a feeding tube inserted. Hours turned into days, then weeks. He developed a blood clot (deep vein thrombosis) in a vein of his right leg. There was no way to surgically remove it, and the Refludan did not dissolve it. The leg began to swell, so incisions were made on both sides of the leg to relieve the pressure and keep the muscle from dying. His right foot began to turn black, then the left foot also.

One day, I happened to notice that Bernett's fingers were turning blue. I mentioned it to the nurse on duty, and that night one of the little Filipino nurses put heat to his hands all night long. The next morning Bernett's fingers were pink again. Had the nurse not done this, he might have lost some fingers. (However, months later, the tips of them eventually sloughed off.)

An army of doctors and nurses worked night and day to save Bernett's life and, if possible, his legs. For several weeks, his very survival was in question. To quote one of the doctors, "We are in trench warfare."

The doctors drained the fluid from Bernett's lungs, and his kidneys started functioning again. But the platelets—it seemed they would never start rebuilding again.

One day, I found myself praying, "Lord, you know I can't do without him!" Immediately realizing that was a selfish prayer, I said, "I'm sorry, Lord. Whatever is best for Bernett. Your will be done." I could not find words for my future prayers, but depended on Romans 8:26-27, which says, "Likewise the Spirit also helpeth our infirmities: for we know not what we should pray for as we ought: but the Spirit itself maketh intercession for us with groanings which cannot be uttered. And he that searcheth the hearts knoweth what is the mind of the Spirit, because he maketh intercession for the saints according to the will of God." The very next verse, Romans 8:28 ("And we know that all things work together for good to them that love God, to them who are the called according to his purpose"), is my life verse.

The ICU daily visiting hours were every two hours. I rarely left the hospital at first, sleeping in the ICU waiting room many nights. Family and friends often stayed with me. With the permission of the hospital, my children brought our RV to the hospital parking lot, so that I could sleep there without having to drive in the dark to a motel. That allowed me to stay at the hospital from 6:00 a.m. to 10:00 p.m. The only three times that I left the hospital grounds were (1) Joel and Sandra Wakeland took me to lunch one day, (2) John and I went to Walmart to get some things for Bernett, and (3) John drove me to get my hair done. (Unfortunately, while we were on the way, a hospital nurse called saying they needed my signature on the permission form for another procedure, and we had to turn around and hurry back.)

During this time, I really struggled with Bernett's slow progress. One night, as I went to my Bible, I just opened it randomly. I needed a word from the Lord. My Bible fell open to Zechariah 4, and I scanned down the page. My eyes suddenly fixed on verse 10, and I read, "For who hath despised the day of small things?" A sudden feeling of relief swept over me, and from then on, I was able to rest in the Lord, knowing that He had all things under His control. Progress would be slow, but it was still progress!

One of the hardest things I have ever had to do was to sign the permission form so they could amputate Bernett's right leg below the knee. I knew I had no choice; it was the only way to save his life. Otherwise, the infection would have spread throughout his body. A week after that surgery, they closed the flap on that leg.

As Bernett began to wake up, it fell to me to tell him that his leg had been amputated. The anesthetic was slow in wearing off, and a medication they were giving him affected his memory, so I had to tell him several days in a row, which was very difficult.

Less than a month later, the doctors amputated a portion of Bernett's left foot, hoping to save the heel. During that surgery, they discovered that the muscle in that heel was dead, so a week later, that leg was also amputated below the knee. The next morning, Bernett's temperature was normal for the first time in weeks. Eventually, he was moved to a room, and then to the swing bed section of the hospital.

Routine bypass surgery had turned into two bypass surgeries and two below-the-knee amputations. During his time in the hospital, Bernett had a total of nine surgeries or procedures that required an anesthetic. He would just begin to awaken from one anesthetic when they would have to give him another one. He was given the equivalent of thirty-three pints of blood during his stay in the hospital, and that, plus all the many medications he was given—and most of all, the good Lord—is all that kept him going until his body finally started to make platelets again. He was in ICU for forty-one days and on the ventilator over a month. The trach and feeding tube were finally removed before he went to rehab.

Bernett had entered the hospital for the first surgery on February 20, 2001, and he was finally transferred to rehab on April 30, 2001, at ten thirty in the evening. I went home the next morning and slept in my own bed that night. I drove down to see Bernett every day at three o'clock, when therapy was over and visiting hours started. Every day he was waiting for me in the lobby in his wheelchair. He was able to go home May 18, 2001.

There were many things that kept me going during this storm. I knew I had to be strong for my husband. Any sign of fear or doubt on my part could have adversely affected his medical progress. I assured him repeatedly that we would conquer this together, that whatever came, we would do what we had to do together. The many friends who came by and helped in numerous ways, the stacks of beautiful get well cards, the gifts, the flowers, and most of all, the many prayers from those dear ones all the way from Georgia to the west coast and to China, these all came together to help us get through this trial. But what helped most of all was the knowledge that the Lord was in control and was there with me.

A favorite quotation, which always hung in Bernett's mother's kitchen, kept coming to my mind: "Sometimes God stills the storm, but sometimes He stills His child and lets the storm rage." Somehow, while this storm was raging all around me, God kept me still and gave me the strength to keep going. Shortly after we came home, I felt I should enlarge on this quotation and try to set it to music. It had meant so much to me that I felt I should share it with others. The words came quickly, and so did the melody. I wish I knew to whom to credit the original quotation. (See Appendix A for the lyrics to "Sometimes God Calms the Storm.")

Chapter 21

Life with Prosthetic Legs

Our schedule, when Bernett finally came home, was rather busy. There were doctors' appointments practically every week, along with physical therapy at Crosby Memorial Hospital in Picayune three times a week for about six months. After his physical therapy ended, Bernett went to The Cornerstone (our local health and fitness center) to exercise with the equipment twice a week.

Two months after Bernett left rehab, we saw a prosthetist, who fitted him for artificial legs. Dr. Parr told him, "Now I don't really expect you to walk. Just try to stand up." With the aid of a walker, Bernett not only stood but walked about twelve feet. Dr. Parr was really amazed at his ability to do that. Bernett had always had excellent balance, and it really stood him in good stead.

At first, Bernett used a manual wheelchair. I had seen a man at the grocery store parking lot use a lift to put a wheelchair into the trunk of his car. We asked around and discovered there was a man in our area who could install a small lift in a car, so we bought one for our car. It really saved my back. Later, when Bernett got an electric wheelchair, our minivan was fitted with a lift for it.

He graduated to using a four-wheeled walker with brakes, then two canes, and finally only one cane. When Bernett was determined to go somewhere, there was no stopping him. Sometimes he would stand up and walk into the next room, totally forgetting to use a cane.

We started going out to lunch daily, as that was a chance to get him out of the house. When we went out to eat, people would open and hold doors for Bernett. He would still try to open the door by himself, and I could tell that he was uncomfortable with anyone doing something for him—Bernett had always been the one doing for others. I sensed his discomfort, and one day I asked him, "Does it make you feel uncomfortable when someone tries to help you?"

"Yes," he said, "I just don't know what to do."

"You just smile and say, 'Thank you,'" I replied, "because people want to help you, and if you don't let them, then you are robbing them of being a blessing to someone else."

He finally relaxed and was able to gratefully acknowledge help from others.

People were amazed when they found out that Bernett was using artificial legs; they just assumed that he had knee problems. Several people at church told me how they had tears in their eyes the first time he was able to help with the Lord's Supper. Bernett was a walking miracle, and God was the only reason that he was still here!

One lady shared with me that when her uncle lost a leg, he just sat down in a wheelchair and gave up. Bernett was made of sterner stuff. If he didn't know how to do something, he would go to the library and find a book and figure it out. Shortly after we moved to Picayune, we had a separate garage built, and we converted the original garage into a room. Bernett did the brickwork and installed a large window to close the opening.

Fortunately for us, the house we purchased just outside of Picayune had no steps and had very wide doors and halls. (My stepfather had used a wheelchair, so we always avoided buying houses with steps.) The only thing we had to do was to remove a couple of doors and enlarge the bathroom doorway in the master bedroom. Two of the men from the church did the work and built small ramps at the front door and patio door. John and Eileen rearranged our bedroom furniture so Bernett could pull his wheelchair up right beside the bed and also access his dresser drawers. We placed a low rack in the front of his closet for his pants. With his reacher, he was able to access his shirts on the top rack. We had a bench to go in the tub and a handheld showerhead. That made it possible for Bernett to shower and dress himself.

Each night, Bernett had to remove his legs, wash the leg liners, and hang them up on their stands before he went to bed. I washed the liners for him at first, but one night I was a little later going to check on him. He had washed them all by himself and was already in bed. I realized then that I must let him do as much for himself as possible. If something happened to me, he needed to be pretty much self-sufficient. As time went on, it just became routine for him.

I would always be nearby if needed to help him at any time. Around five o'clock in the afternoon, Bernett would head to the bedroom, take off his legs to be more comfortable, get in bed, and watch TV. He used a transfer board to get from the wheelchair to the bed and vice versa. (Since my stepfather had used a sliding board [transfer board], I was already familiar with its use and was not anxious about Bernett using it. My mother set a good example for me. I knew if she could do what was needed to help my stepfather, I could do the same for my husband.)

At first, we had a problem trying to find pants that were wide enough in the legs (the bottom had to be ten inches) in order for him to be able to pull them up as far as he could to put on or adjust his legs. We found some at Sears that had zippers in the bottom of the legs, but then we found some jeans (Carhartt brand) that had legs wide enough. From then on, we bought those for him.

We purchased hand controls for our vehicles so Bernett could drive, and in November after the surgery, he helped drive on a trip to Oklahoma to attend my sister-in-law's funeral.

The following spring in 2002, my left leg broke, and I fell, dislocating my right shoulder. I was taken to Slidell Memorial Hospital. They put my shoulder back in place that night, and the next day they surgically put a rod in my leg and a pin in my hip. After a few days, I was transferred to rehab. Each day, Bernett came to visit me. My brother, Gordon, came and stayed with him during this time. After I came home, Bernett said, "I don't know how y'all did that—going to the hospital every day." It really opened his eyes to what all of us had gone through when he was in the hospital.

Bernett's biggest regret was that he couldn't work in the yard and garden as much as he had before. (When we moved here, forty years ago, he planted trees, flowers, azaleas, and blueberry bushes. Every year, he planted a garden with tomatoes, cucumbers, squash, corn, and watermelons.) He now planted tomatoes and cucumbers in grow boxes and large pots. His four-wheeled scooter made it easier for him to tend to them. With the scooter, he could also go to the mailbox, pick up the newspaper, and take out the garbage.

I was okay with most everything Bernett tried, but the first time he got on his new hand-controlled riding mower, I sat in the house and cried for about an hour! All I could think of was *What if he should fall off?* The tears I had kept pent-up ever since he went in the hospital all came out that day in a flood of relief. Tears of worry and concern, then thankfulness and relief. God had spared his life, and he was able to walk and still do much that he normally did. He could mow the grass and even get on the large tractor to bushhog the rest of the property. When he wanted to clear the yard of sticks, he would attach a small trailer to the mower and ride around the yard, picking up sticks with a grabber.

After losing his legs, Bernett didn't dwell on what he couldn't do, choosing instead to focus on what he still could do. Our church offered an evening meal on Wednesday nights before the prayer meeting, and Bernett and I collected the money from the people when they came to eat. Also, once a month, we counted the money from the Sunday offerings and got it ready to be deposited in the bank.

We had a chiming clock above our couch, and once a week, Bernett would take the pillows off the couch and climb up on it to wind the clock. I always cringed when he did that; I was so afraid he might fall.

We discovered that the Senior Center in Picayune offered painting classes. Since we had been watching various painting programs on TV, we decided that we would take lessons. We enjoyed learning to paint with acrylics, and each of us finished several paintings. The following year we were extremely busy and gradually dropped out of the class. Bernett was working on a painting of the Old Mill of Pigeon Forge, Tennessee, before he died.

There were times that we got some humor out of the situation. One day, when Bernett and I were out eating, I moved my leg under the table and accidentally kicked him.

"I'm sorry," I said. "I didn't mean to kick you."

"That's okay," he replied. "I didn't feel it."

Several times, during medical exams, a doctor would ask, "Any swelling?" as he automatically felt of Bernett's ankles. Bernett and I would look at each other and grin. Sheepishly, the doctor would say, "Oh, I forgot!" We had a good laugh about it.

Of course, we made numerous trips to the prosthetist for adjustments, and Bernett had to have new artificial legs made several times. Once, on a trip to Oklahoma, one of his own legs became irritated. I checked the inside of the prosthetic leg, and there was a tiny sharply pointed spot sticking out. I promptly went to my purse, pulled out an emery board, and smoothed the point completely down. He didn't have any more problems with his leg on that trip.

Sometimes at night, Bernett's legs would start hurting with phantom pain. He never complained about it but would often wait until it became severe before asking for a pill. Consequently, it would take much longer for the medication to take effect.

Several years after his surgeries, I asked Bernett what his thinking was when he was told he had lost both legs. He said, "Well, I just remember those guys on TV walking on extremely tall stilts. So, I figured if they could walk on those, surely I could walk on legs." (After we moved to Picayune, Bernett made some stilts, walked around the yard on them, and taught Margaret how to walk on them.)

For nine years Bernett used only a cane for balance when walking, but after he had two bad falls—hitting his head both times—we knew it was time for him to always use the walker.

Chapter 22

Alaskan Cruise

Bernett had always wanted to go on an Alaskan cruise. Holland America always sent us their cruise information, and we noticed there was an Alaskan cruise that Dr. Adrian Rogers was going to be on. When our good friend Frankie Wyatt heard that Dr. Rogers would be on the ship, she said, "Oh, I'd love to go on that one too." We were not a part of his tour group but would be able to visit with him occasionally.

So, in August 2003, Bernett, Frankie, and I went on a Holland America Alaskan Inside Passage Cruise. We flew into Vancouver, where we had a couple of days before the cruise began. On the first day, we took a bus tour of the city, which included Chinatown and Stanley Park. In the park, we were able to get out and walk around. A Chinese man was playing his erhu (Chinese violin), and I bought a cassette tape of his music.

On our first day in Vancouver, we ate breakfast in the hotel dining area. Not thinking, I ordered orange juice. When the check came, I realized everything was priced separately. The glass of orange juice was six dollars. We decided after that we should find a cheaper place to eat.

We had seen a McDonald's across the street, and the night before, Frankie had pointed out a sign in the hotel lobby that read "McDonald's" with an arrow pointing. At noon, we didn't think to look for the arrow. (There was an underground tunnel connecting the hotel and McDonald's.) Bernett was in a hurry, and he was ready to cross the street. There was a light rain falling, so I said, "Wait a minute, Bernett. I need to put my rain hat on." Well, he was out the door and on his way. Frankie and I hurried to catch up. After a good lunch, we saw a sign directing us to the underground tunnel, and we took that back to the hotel.

The following day we boarded a ferry for a day trip to Victoria Island. There, buses took us to Butchart Gardens, which had been created in an abandoned gravel pit. We walked down and around the well-kept grounds, enjoying the beautiful flowers, trees, and shrubs. No matter what time of year you visit, there are always flowers blooming. They are just exquisite. It was the highlight of our trip.

Boarding the *Volendam* the next morning, we sailed for a couple of days to Juneau. At the beginning of the cruise, we were provided information about the different tours that were available. We chose tours that didn't require a lot of walking, since Bernett and I were both using canes at that time.

In Juneau, we took a bus tour, which included Glacier Gardens, the Macaulay Salmon Hatchery, and the Mendenhall Glacier. The gardens were formed in an area that had had a landslide. In the process of removing the fallen trees, someone came up with the idea of using huge machines to turn the trunks upside down and pound them into the ground. They added soil to the roots of the trees (which were now high in the air) and planted flowers there. Flowers were planted on the ground as well, and all of them were spectacular.

Our next stop was Skagway, where we took the early morning train ride on the White Pass and Yukon Route Railroad. It was cold outside, but there was a stove in each train car to keep it warm. The scenery as the train wound its way up the mountain was beautiful, with blue skies above, though there was fog down below. When we arrived back in Skagway, the whole mountain was enveloped in fog, so it was good that we had taken the early train.

Next we went to Glacier Bay National Park. Exhibits there explained how glaciers are formed and showed how much this glacier had receded. The ship then sailed to the Margerie Glacier, stopping right in front of it for over an hour. We sat near the windows as we ate lunch and watched while little pieces of the glacier broke off (called ice calving).

Each day after our tour, Bernett went back to the ship to rest, and Frankie and I did a little shopping for things to take back home. Once, upon our return to the ship, we discovered that the gangplank—which had been almost level that morning—was now at a very steep angle. The tide had come in, lifting the ship about ten feet higher. Both Frankie and I had trouble climbing up to the ship, but thankfully, there was a handrail on one side of the gangplank. Inclines—especially steep ones—are very difficult for people with prosthetic legs, so I was really anxious until I got back to our stateroom and discovered that Bernett was there and was alright.

Our last stop before heading back to Vancouver was Ketchikan. We toured the Saxman Native Village with the Totem Park. Entering a theater, we watched a great performance of native Alaskan dances.

The Great Alaskan Lumberjack Show was really fun to watch. They competed in sawing and chopping logs, climbing poles, and ax throwing. For the finale, they had a log rolling contest. While we were sitting in the stands, a bald eagle flew down and perched on a light pole nearby. Everyone just stopped and stared in awe.

We returned to Vancouver, and a bus took us to the airport. As we were waiting to go through customs before boarding the plane for home, Frankie said, "Bernett, if you get a wheelchair, we can go to the head of the line, instead of standing here and waiting." We stood for over an hour, barely inching along, because Bernett wouldn't ask for a wheelchair. No special favors for him! He refused to consider himself handicapped.

We were a little disappointed in the weather the week of our cruise. Most of the time, we had cloudy skies with a little misty rain. Because of this, the scenery was not quite as spectacular as we had hoped. But we had a great time, and I told Bernett I could really learn to enjoy cruising—no cooking, no dishes to wash!

Chapter 23

Tippy

Since Bernett had two artificial legs, he was not as active as he used to be. Consequently, he spent more time sitting in his recliner. I felt that he needed a lapdog to keep his mind off of himself and to have something to care for.

One day on our way home from New Orleans, I asked Bernett, "Do you want to go by the shelter and see if they have a small dog?" He agreed, so we went and looked. They had one really small dog. She was white and had long fur but was cute as she could be. I fell in love with her immediately, and we adopted her. When we walked in the house, Bernett sat down in his chair, and she instantly jumped up in his lap. Clearly, she had been someone's lapdog. We named her Tippy, because she was white all over with a pale golden color tipping her back and head.

After she came to live with us, Tippy quickly adjusted to Bernett's use of a cane and wheelchair. She was just like Bernett's shadow; she went everywhere he did. She would lie in his lap anytime he was in his recliner and look out the back door, hoping to see a squirrel to chase. When he took a nap, she took a nap.

When Bernett went outside and got on his four-wheel scooter, Tippy immediately hopped on the scooter's floor for a ride! If he stopped to pick up a limb or to pick blueberries, she would get off and explore a little (we had several acres, so at first, we let Tippy roam at will). Most of the time, the instant he got back on his scooter she was right there ready to hop back on. Sometimes when he went to get the mail, Bernett would hold Tippy in his arms until they were back inside.

When Tippy was outside, many times she would take off running without paying any attention to where she was going. One day we were leaving the house, driving very slowly, when Tippy suddenly darted out right in front of us. I said, "That's it. We're getting a fence." We fenced in a small portion of our backyard, so she would be safe.

At mealtimes, Bernett would always give Tippy a bite of his food. When we went out to eat, he would save something to take home to her. As the years went by, he brought larger portions—sometimes half his sandwich—home for Tippy.

Apparently, Tippy had never learned to play much as a puppy, but she *would* play with a soft fuzzy ball. Bernett would throw it into the kitchen, and she would run after it and bring it back to him. Her other favorite toy was a flat fuzzy blue bear, which she loved to chew on. Oftentimes, Tippy would get the bear and lie down beside Bernett's chair. He would reach down and grab the bear, and they would play tug-of-war, with Tippy growling playfully. After a few minutes, she was through playing and would flop down on the floor as if exhausted.

In the evening after Bernett had gone into the bedroom, Tippy would curl up in my lap until time for bed.

During Bernett's last few months—especially in the daytime when he was asleep in his chair—Tippy would get down off his lap and come get in mine. She seemed to cling to me more, snuggling up in my lap. I would hold her close, thinking, *Tippy, before too long it will just be you and me.* Somehow, I knew the time was short.

Tippy died at the age of fourteen, a few months after her master left us.

Betty and Bernett in Athens, Greece

Betty and Bernett in Egypt

Bernett and Betty at Butchart Gardens

Betty and Bernett at Mendenhall Glacier

Bernett on his scooter with Tippy

Bernett in his chair with Tippy in his lap

Twenty-fifth wedding anniversary, March 14, 1981

Fortieth wedding anniversary, March 14, 1996

Fiftieth wedding anniversary, March 14, 2006

Sixtieth wedding anniversary, March 14, 2016

Bernett, with his father, Barney, and paternal grandparents, John and Nettie Aceneith Anderson Padgett. Nettie is holding Eileen.

Bernett, with his father and maternal grandmother, Martha Perry Gill Hales. Martha is holding Eileen.

Bernett, with his parents, Barney and Ludie.

Bernett and his sisters, Marjorie Anne and Mary Jean, at Marjorie Anne's seventy-fifth birthday party.

Bernett and Betty's Children

Bernett, Betty, and Eileen

Bernett and Margaret

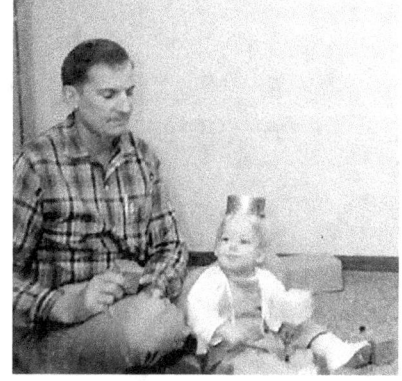

Bernett and John

Grandchildren

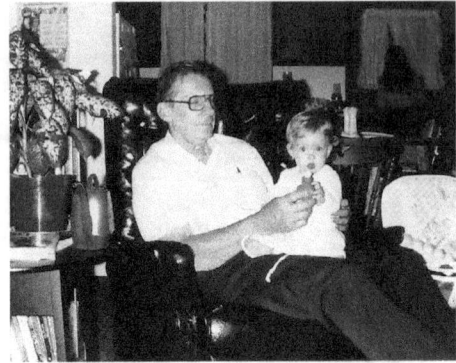

Bernett and Rachel

Bernett and Allison

Bernett and Stephanie   *Bernett and Tiffany*

Great-Grandchildren

Bernett and Joshua

Bernett, Betty, and Jax

Bernett and Tucker

Betty and Wyatt

Bernett and Emma Grace

Betty and Ellie Kate

Bernett and Betty at their home

Chapter 24

Going Home

As Bernett grew older, it became harder and harder for him to do things, such as using the transfer board. He grew weaker and fell more frequently. One of our neighbors, Brad Spiers, came over many times and helped Bernett get up.

Bernett gradually began sleeping more each day. On Monday, February 26, 2018, he was so weak he could not get out of bed. The next morning, I knew I had to get him to a doctor. I gave him a choice. "You can try to get up and get dressed, or we can call 911." With my help, he put his legs on. Determinedly he stood, took a step, and sat in the wheelchair. We repeated this in the bathroom, and he managed to change clothes. He went in his motorized wheelchair to the car, stood, took a step, and got in the car. I had intended to drive to the doctor's office but, on the way, changed my mind and headed for the ER. Bernett was too weak to have to get in and out of the car two times. I got him settled in the hospital, and they began to run tests. Enlarged heart was what they decided. I went home that evening to get some rest.

I was awakened at about one thirty by a phone call from the hospital. The nurse said Bernett had had a little episode, and they had moved him to the cardiac care unit. I asked if he was stable, and the reply was yes. They said they would let me know if there was any change.

About four thirty, the phone rang again, and I was told they were going to transfer Bernett to Forrest General Hospital in Hattiesburg, Mississippi (about an hour away). I dressed quickly, phoned my friend Frankie and Bro. Dan Young (our pastor), and headed to the hospital. Upon arrival, I was told that the "little episode" was that Bernett's heart had stopped twice! The doctors and nurses had worked feverishly on him, doing CPR along with defibrillations, and he was stable at that time. I messaged my daughters, son, and Bernett's sister Mary Jean.

Frankie, Bro. Dan, and I, along with one of the nurses, took Bernett's belongings to the car. The nurse hugged me and said, "He is so funny." Apparently, Bernett had been joking with the nurses.

Following the ambulance, Frankie drove me to Hattiesburg, and Bro. Dan followed us in his car. He said, "I couldn't let you two 'wild women' drive all that way by yourselves at this hour." Bless him!

Upon arrival at Forrest General, Bernett was immediately taken to ICU. Eileen arrived soon afterward, and Marjorie Anne and her daughter Elizabeth came from Magee. John was on the road, driving from Tennessee, and he arrived in the afternoon. Margaret, who now lived in Virginia, flew in that night.

Our granddaughters Rachel and Allison came to see him that evening. Giving the hospital staff both of our cell phone numbers, John and I spent Wednesday night in a motel in Hattiesburg to be nearby. Bernett had already made the decision "Do not resuscitate" in his living will, and the family notified the hospital of his wishes.

On Thursday morning, Mary Jean and Marjorie Anne (both registered nurses) came, and we talked with the doctors in the ICU. The echocardiogram that they had done on Wednesday showed that Bernett's heart was only working at 30 percent capacity. The doctors wanted to do more tests. If they did an angiogram, there was a chance that Bernett's kidneys would fail. I asked, "If you find out what's wrong, can you fix it?" The answer was no.

The doctor told Bernett that they would be moving him to a room soon. As we approached his bed, we suddenly realized he was praying out loud. The only words we understood were "safe travel." We don't know if he was praying for himself or for family members.

We talked with Bernett a while, and he said, "I need to get out of this bed."

"I don't think the nurses would like that," Mary Jean commented.

"Oh, you just don't know how to handle them." he said with a grin.

We all had a good laugh, which broke the tension in the room.

After Eileen and Margaret arrived, the family discussed the pros and cons, and decided against the angiogram or any other test. We didn't want to risk Bernett's having to go on dialysis (there was no reason to put him through that, after all that he had already been through). He would not have survived another surgery.

Thus, began the vigil. We drove back and forth to Forrest General each day. Bernett was so weak, he was unable to feed himself at first, but by Saturday he had regained some strength and was more alert. His chest was very sore from the defibrillations that the doctors had done. He said it felt like he had been beaten up. Mary Jean and Marjorie Anne came as often as they could. Our granddaughter Tiffany visited him on Sunday.

Each morning when I arrived, Bernett had a question ready for me, such as, "Did you bring my legs?" "Did you bring my shoes?" and one day, "Did you bring my boots?" (He didn't have any boots.) Bernett really wanted to get up out of that bed!

On Friday a student nurse entered his room and asked my permission for her and some fellow student nurses to practice how to bathe an immobile patient and change his bed. I said yes, and they promptly went to work. They bathed him gently and, with the assistance of their supervisor, learned how to change the bed with him in it. They had to turn him twice in order to do that. Before she left the room, one of the student nurses gently combed his hair.

By Sunday we were advised by hospital staff that Bernett needed to be moved to hospice in Picayune. We were very concerned about having to move him in his frail condition. Later that day a dear friend, Sarah Criswell, made some calls and learned that there was an opening in hospice in Highland Community Hospital, our local hospital. We were thankful there was a place nearby to move him to.

On Sunday afternoon Margaret and I left the hospital earlier than usual to get a little more rest. Just before we left, I kissed Bernett on the forehead and told him that I loved him. As we were driving home, my back began to hurt, and the thought flashed through my mind, *I don't know how much longer I can make this one-hour drive.* At the same time, I was praying, *Lord, don't let him suffer. Help us to know what* to do.

Since I have a landline, I always turn my cell phone off when I go to bed, so John got the call about one thirty Monday morning. Bernett's heart had finally given out. They said he took a couple of breaths and then was gone. The Lord was merciful and gave us a few more days with him. Thank you, Lord, that he didn't suffer and that he didn't have to be moved again. God made that decision for us.

My children and I talked about our reactions. We knew that we would miss him terribly, but we had done most of our grieving in 2001 when Bernett had almost died. We are so thankful for those seventeen extra years we had with him. I could not be selfish enough to want him to linger on and probably be bedfast. He wouldn't have wanted that.

At the age of eighty-seven, the love of my life went to be with his Lord and Savior Jesus Christ. Those last years, Bernett had written two songs about heaven (which I had set to music) and was working on another. At the funeral, Bro. Brad Replogle (our Minister of Music) sang "More than Wonderful." Bro. Dan officiated and read one of Bernett's songs ("A Savior Came from Heaven"). He then read Psalms 127 and 128 and spoke about building a family that honors and glorifies God. Our son, John, sang the other of his father's songs ("I'm Going Home"). As the lyrics indicated, Bernett was ready to go and really looking forward to his heavenly home. (See Appendices B and C for the lyrics to Bernett's two songs.)

The Mississippi Chapter of the Patriot Guard Riders of America escorted the funeral procession to the cemetery. Officers from Keesler Air Force Base folded the flag that had draped his coffin and presented it to me. Taps was played, and Bro. Dan read John 14:1-3 (where Jesus says that He is going to prepare a place for us) and then prayed. After the graveside service, we went back to the church for a meal with family and friends, and then home.

As we turned into our driveway, all the azaleas that Bernett had planted years ago were in full bloom. Our whole yard was a riot of color. It was as if everything bloomed all at once just for him.

Epilogue

Bernett loved the Lord very much, and he was faithful in everything he did to further God's kingdom. Our children grew up loving the Lord, and all are serving Him in some capacity. We are very proud of them.

Eileen worked for the navy and is now retired. She is married and has three daughters and one stepdaughter. Her oldest daughter, Rachel, is a school counselor. Allison is a speech pathologist. Tiffany is a high school English teacher, and Noelle is a registered nurse. Eileen has four grandsons and three granddaughters.

Margaret is the owner of TABLELAND PRESS LLC. She is married and has one daughter, Stephanie, who is a very good writer.

John works for the city of Murfreesboro, Tennessee, as a videographer and has won several nationwide awards for his work. He is also an excellent wildlife photographer.

Appendix A

"Sometimes God Calms the Storm"
by Betty Hendricks Padgett

Sometimes God calms the storm,
And keeps us from all harm,
But sometimes God calms His child
And lets the storm rage.
Days may be dark and drear,
Nights be tinged with fear,
But peace and rest will come
With trust in the Lord.
For God is still on His throne.
He will care for His own.
Sometimes God calms the storm,
Sometimes God calms the storm,
But sometimes God calms His child
And lets the storm rage.

Thank you, glorious Lord
For promises in your Word
For blessed assurance that You
Are still in control.
Give us listening ears
That we may always hear
Your still small voice
Whenever you may call.

For You are still on Your throne.
You will care for Your own.
Sometimes You calm the storm.
Sometimes You calm the storm.
But sometimes You calm Your child
And let the storm rage.

Sometimes God calms the storm.
Sometimes God calms the storm.
But sometimes God calms His child
And lets the storm rage.

Appendix B

"A Savior Came from Heaven"
By Lacy Bernett Padgett

A Savior came from heaven
To save men from their sin.
He taught, did many miracles,
But men rejected Him.

They nailed Him to a cross,
Then laid Him in a tomb.
They said unto themselves,
"Now that's the end of Him."

The grave, it could not keep Him.
He arose on the third day
And went back to His Father
To rule and reign always.

When the Lord calls me home,
And I see Him face to face,
I'll thank Him for His great love
And for His saving grace.

I'll walk all over God's heaven.
I'll walk those streets of gold.
I'll stroll up Prayer Boulevard
To Hallelujah Square.

I'll join the heavenly choir
Singing praises to my King
For His great love for me.
Hallelujah, what a day that will be!

Appendix C

"I'm Going Home"
By Lacy Bernett Padgett

While traveling down this road of life, some trials I have seen.
And when it seems I can't go on, on Jesus I must lean.
He picks me up and carries me through all the storms of life.
For Jesus is my Savior. I place my trust in Him.

Chorus:
I'm going home to be with Christ my Savior.
And He has promised me a mansion there.
For I am His, and He is mine forever.
I'm going home, what glory that will be.

I'm going where sorrow and sickness is no more.
The blind can see, the dumb can speak, and the lame can walk.
Where streets are paved with gold as far as eye can see.
And Jesus is the light throughout eternity.

I hear my Father calling, "Come home, my
   child, come home.
Your work on earth is over; it's now time to
   come home.
I'm sending you my angels to lead you on
   your way.
Your loved ones here are waiting to welcome
   you home."

Receive this FREE eBook

Learn how God works in your life by exploring how He directed the paths of eight biblical people.

In addition, you will receive devotionals, Bible quizzes, reviews of Christian books, and the latest news from TABLELAND PRESS LLC.

Download your free PDF today at
www.tablelandpress.com

You Might Also Enjoy...

Now I Know His Name
by Frankie Willingham Wyatt
with Margaret Sorensen

Follow the adventures of Frankie Willingham Wyatt, a sixty-two-year-old widow, who answered God's call to share the gospel in China.

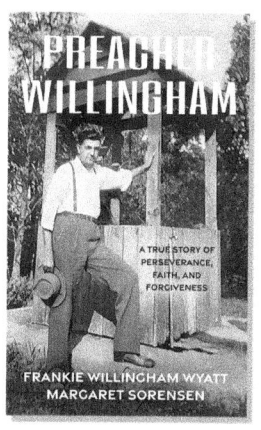

Preacher Willingham
by Frankie Willingham Wyatt
and Margaret Sorensen

Kidnapped, deprived, and beaten. Discover how Wesley Frank Willingham turned a childhood filled with hardships and abuse into a life of victory that glorified God.

Available online where books and ebooks are sold.
Visit our website at www.tablelandpress.com

www.ingramcontent.com/pod-product-compliance
Lightning Source LLC
Chambersburg PA
CBHW072017110526
44592CB00012B/1345